NOSTRADAMUS
PROPHECIES FOR WOMEN

NOSTRADAMUS
PROPHECIES FOR WOMEN

Manuela Dunn Mascetti
&
Peter Lorie

SIMON & SCHUSTER

New York London Toronto Sydney Tokyo Singapore

SIMON & SCHUSTER
Simon & Schuster Building
Rockefeller Center
1230 Avenue of the Americas
New York, New York 10020

A LABYRINTH BOOK
Copyright © 1995 Labyrinth Publishing (UK) Ltd
Text copyright © 1995 Manuela Dunn Mascetti and Peter Lorie

N O S T R A D A M U S – P R O P H E C I E S   F O R   W O M E N
was produced by Labyrinth Publishing (UK) Ltd
Art Editor – Patricia McCarver
Design by DW Design
Typesetting by DW Design in London, England

Printed in Italy
1 3 5 7 9 10 8 6 4 2

Lorie, Peter
     Nostradamus : prophecies for women / Peter Lorie and Manuela Dunn Mascetti.
     p. cm.
     Includes index.
     ISBN 0-671-89656-3

    I. Nostradamus, 1503–1566. 2. Prophecies (Occultism) 3. Women—Social conditions—
Forecasting. 4. Twenty-first century—Forecasts. I. Mascetti, Manuela Dunn. II. Nostradamus,
1503–1566. Prophéties. English. Selections. III. Title.

    BF1815.N8L57 1995
    133.3–dc20   94-45227
                                         CIP

CONTENTS

INTRODUCTION

WOMEN THEN

"Civilized" life—that is, human life under patriarchal control—has always been miserable...
Marilyn French, Beyond Power

MICHEL DE NOSTRADAME, the prophet and physician, lived in the first half of the sixteenth century, at a time in European history when women were still securely under the domination of men in almost all respects—social, political and religious.

Women enjoyed no financial or political independence. They were governed by the male-oriented rules of heredity in a society which treated them as inferior in law and custom. Patriarchal control had infested every corner of the civilized world and certainly there was a great deal of misery, especially for women, as a result of it.

The predominant religious influence at the time in Europe was Catholicism. A massively powerful God, represented on Earth by a rich, ritualistic Church led by a single male figure, the Pope, provided the personal, moral and indeed social laws that governed the mind, body and spirit.

Dictatorial, essentially warlike monarchs, sanctioned by the Church, presided over authoritarian regimes which restricted the ways in which individuals undertook their day-to-day lives. All this was almost totally male-dominated, and gave rise to the burning of witches at the stake for "crimes" that could be as minor as a local act of feminine healing, or even the choice made by a single woman to live alone.

The great schism brought about in the Church by the Protestant Reformation in no way improved the lot of women. Suspicion and fear were everywhere, and women suffered most.

This state of severe confinement, suffered by women at the hands of men, reached a peak under the so-called "Inquisition" or "Holy Office," a tribunal of the Church originally established in 1229 to hunt down and suppress heresy. By the sixteenth century the Inquisition operated in France, Italy,

Opposite: A fifteenth-century painting of St. Dominic burning the Albigensian scriptures, by Pedro Berruguete, in the Prado, Madrid. The burning of books and the persecution of heresy by Church and State drove dissident ideas underground.

Below: The demonization of women. A nineteenth-century mural from the Rila Monastery in Bulgaria, depicting witches and devils.

Spain, and the Holy Roman Empire, and was especially active after the Reformation. Heresy was any form of "deviant" behavior that it chose to define as such. The definition of these forms of "crime" against God was left in the hands of the inquisitors—monks drawn from the mendicant orders, assisted by a jury composed of clerics and laymen—and the powers to exact punishment were placed in the same grasp, the grasp of very often fanatical male individuals whose sole task was to rid the land of any influence that might be regarded as "impure." This Holy Office was later extended also to include the new lands of America and still exists today, renamed the "Sacred Congregation for the Doctrine of the Faith" in 1965, to deal with matters of ecclesiastical discipline.

In the kind of tribal cleansing which took place women were considered "evil," quite literally. The Church regarded them as possessing, as an important part of their natural function, the purpose of diverting men from their proper path to God. This "engaging" capability, which was seen in a negative light, took the form of a sensuous, sexual influence which the pious male was supposed assiduously to avoid. Added to this the female "irrational" or instinctive nature, which was associated with "magic," again in a negative sense, brought further exacerbation because it gave rise to inexplicable healing powers and an understanding of the human environment in a way that was at odds with the laws of patriarchal, religious and sexually repressive propriety.

Below: An undated woodcut published in Camille Flammarion's *L'Astronomie*, showing man's desire to look out into the universe.

Opposite: A colored woodcut of Nostradamus, c. 1850.

Further problems were associated with feminine nature because of certain passages in the Bible that were interpreted as being anti-women. Many of these passages were, it seems in retrospect, "deliberately" interpreted by the Church in this way simply to fit in with the overall attitude towards women that was developed by a male-dominated society.

All this is today something of a cliché, though the patriarchal attitudes that existed then are by no means absent in the twentieth century. In Nostradamus' time the misogyny of society was overwhelming, making it all the more remarkable that this unique prophet had such insight into how the situation might change in the future.

THE PROPHET

ICHEL DE NOSTREDAME (1503-66) was born in St. Rémy, Provence, into a Jewish family which had converted to Catholicism to avoid religious persecution by the Church. France had officially expelled its Jews in 1394, and converts were regarded with suspicion, particularly those arriving from Spain and Portugal. The institution of the Inquisition in France in 1558 officially constituted a formal method of punishing heresy. Nostradamus transgressed the law of the Church in more ways than one—first as a "New Christian" (one who had converted from Judaism) and second as an alchemist, astrologer and prophet, performing activities which were considered to be in the realm of God alone. What was worse, he became famous for these transgressions. But it was not until towards the end of his life that he was actively pursued by the Inquisition. As a child, nevertheless, he was a "New Christian," and therefore learned from his family the need for caution.

Nostradamus was introduced to the essentially pagan studies of alchemy, astrology and the occult at an early age. He later trained as a medical doctor at

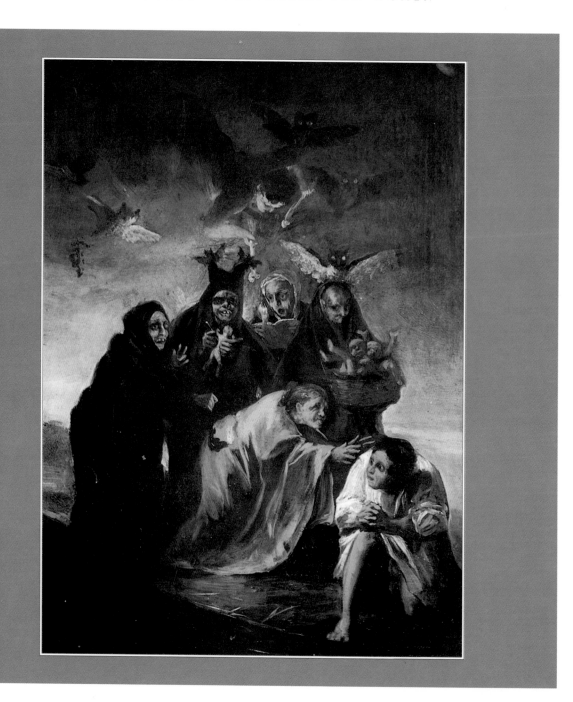

Opposite: Goya's *Notturno con streghe,* "Witches at night," from the Museo Lazaro Galdiano in Madrid.

the University of Montpellier, mainly because his uncle and grandfather, who were his early teachers, knew that a knowledge of astrology would not guarantee him a secure career and income, and, in any event, could get him into trouble with the religious authorities.

In the sixteenth century, astrology and astronomy were not regarded as separate subjects, but studied together as "Celestial Science." As a young man, Nostradamus undertook detailed studies of the stars and planets during his free time from his work as a student doctor. His knowledge of the way the heavens moved in cyclic, repetitive motions would form the corroborative basis for his attempts to substantiate his prophetic gift.

Once through the college of medicine, the young doctor quickly involved himself in the most urgent task of the age—finding a cure for the dread bubonic plague that periodically swept across France and killed shockingly high numbers of the human population. His cures were remarkably successful and consisted of using natural remedies such as dried and crushed rose petals in capsules placed under the tongue of the sufferer to release Vitamin C into the blood.

One of the most remarkable aspects of Nostradamus' character was his advanced view of human nature. His coupling of intrinsic wisdom with insights into the future was not to be found in even the most talented individuals of his age. In his *Centuries*—prophetic rhymed quatrains, written between 1555 and 1558—he undertook subjects and examined issues that would not be remotely considered by his contemporaries as having any relevance to, or likelihood in, their age. Events predicted include those of political change such as the birth and death of modern Communism—a concept so far removed from the reality of his own time that it must have seemed to him almost completely alien to the world. Other subjects that his prophecies cover include alliances between America and what used to be the USSR, the instances of war throughout the world in the twentieth century and beyond, the presence of what he termed "antichrists"—individuals whom he actually named, such as Napoleon and Hitler—and many other events

15

Opposite: Burning at the stake of Jews. Colored woodcut by Michael Wolgemut in the *Liber Chronicarum,* Nuremberg, 1493.

that have actually occurred. Nostradamus was probably the most effective prophet in the history of the human race.

He also made much of the growing power of women and of the restoration of the sexual equality of antiquity, a subject, as we have already seen, which was about as alien to the sixteenth century as the concept of television!

Nostradamus foresaw flying machines, nuclear wars, alien visitors, space travel, the United States of America—subjects so remote to his time that such visions could only have arisen through some extraordinary gift. And in the following pages we will come closer to the one, perhaps most important, issue that was contained in that vision: the paradigm shift that will place women in most of the positions of power throughout the civilized world during the years of the twentieth and twenty-first centuries—specifically the years around the end of the old millennium and the beginning of the new one.

The very nature of Nostradamus' gift made him highly suspect to the Church authorities later in his life, and he was hounded by the Inquisition for at least the last decade before he died. For this reason the verses of his prophecies are obscurely written and heavily camouflaged with ancient languages, strange references to contemporary events, which act as metaphors for future significance, as well as anagrams. This effort was partly to avoid detection during his lifetime, and also to keep the prophecies "pure" until the stage in human affairs was reached when mankind could be mature enough to see its own future and so relate to it with wisdom.

In the following pages, therefore, we will "translate" the complex verses freely. In order to make the reader's task more pleasant and easier to handle, the verse will first be provided in the literal translation and then interpreted in modern English. It is hoped that this will clarify and elucidate.

The Latinized name Nostradamus means "our Lady," an appropriate name for someone whose life was continuously influenced by several important and sometimes powerful women. His predictions are peppered with interest in the various "royal" women who peopled the period between his life and ours, and go on to pay attention also to women in power in our future.

A highly important influence during his later life was Catherine de' Medici, one of the most powerful single individuals to rule a major part of Europe in the sixteenth century.

CATHERINE DE' MEDICI AND NOSTRADAMUS

The young lion will beat the older on the field of
battle in single conflict. His eye will be pierced
through a cage of gold, two wounds made into one,
and then he dies a dreadful death.

CENTURY 1: 35

CATERINA DE' MEDICI was born in Florence, Italy, on April 13, 1519. She became Queen Consort to Henry II of France on his accession to the throne in 1547 and then, upon his death (during a tournament predicted by Nostradamus three years before), Regent of France during the minority of her son Charles IX, from 1560 to 1563. She continued to wield great influence until 1574. Of her ten children seven, the "Valois Children," survived, and three became Kings of France. Among her remarkably diverse talents she was heralded as one of the greatest architectural designers in French history and was responsible for the Palace of the Tuileries and the unfinished Château de Chenonceaux, among other remarkable buildings.

In the royal, male-dominated age of France of the sixteenth century it was not possible for Catherine to rule alone, and although she effectively controlled

Right: El Greco's portrait of the Grand Inquisitor, Cardinal Fernando Niño de Guevara, c. 1569. The power of the Spanish Inquisition was a matter of great concern to Nostradamus, as he was personally threatened by it.

Opposite: Catherine de' Medici, Queen of France, daughter of Lorenzo II de' Medici of Florence.

the country as Regent and Queen Mother during the rest of her life, the authority of the French throne was vested in the hands first of her son Francis II, and later her of other son Charles IX. This was a time of religious and political conflict, caused by the growth of Calvinism and compounded by noble factionalism. Much power was actually wielded by the Guise brothers, François and Charles de Lorraine—ardent Catholic aristocrats who attempted to reduce what they perceived as royal laxity and to institute the religious passion of the Spanish and other European thrones controlled by the Church. It was Charles, who was Cardinal of Lorraine, who introduced the Inquisition into France in 1558. Catherine therefore fought frequent battles, both real and political, against the Church, and secretly remained passionately attached to pre-Christian beliefs epitomized by astrology, occultism, alchemy and what was then seen as black magic. While publicly displaying a devoutly Catholic face, she always kept pace with the ancient beliefs, and this was how she came into contact with Nostradamus.

The story began shortly before the death of her husband, Henry II, in 1559. He died from a wound to his head during a tournament joust, an event predicted by Nostradamus three years before. Nostradamus' *Centuries* had begun to be published in 1555, by which time he already enjoyed considerable fame throughout France because of almanacs which he had previously published, giving astrolog-

ical predictions and verses for each month of the coming year. These were written as "quatrains," and they became bestsellers, thereby bringing him to Catherine's notice. She had taken seriously the verse predicting her husband's death, and had shown it to King Henry prior to the tournament, begging him not to take part.

Nostradamus was summoned from his home in Salon, Provence, and asked to explain the prediction. His journey—one that today could be made in an hour—took a month, and that speed was possible only because of fresh horses supplied by the Queen at various stages along the route. He was treated somewhat as a famous actor might be today, arriving in the French capital city and at Court amidst great excitement and circumstance.

At his private meeting with Catherine, Nostradamus enjoyed her great enthusiasm as she raised many issues concerning the future, on which the prophet gave his advice. Henry II, on the other hand, was entirely uninterested in this strange man from Salon, and departed soon after Nostradamus had tactfully explained quatrain 35 from *Century* 1 to him, attempting not to upset him too seriously.

In 1559, sure enough, the prophetic verse proved to be true and uncannily accurate in its detail. King Henry II was killed in single combat in a jousting tournament by a younger man, the lance piercing the

helmet and entering his head. He died in great agony, "a dreadful death."

Following this fulfillment of his words, Nostradamus became immensely famous throughout Europe. With the fame came notoriety and greater pressure from the Catholic authorities, who now firmly believed him to be influenced by the devil, for surely, they argued, knowledge of the future lay only in the hands of God. Nostradamus was even blamed for the death of the King of France.

THE MAGICAL MASTER

ATHERINE WAS BUT ONE OF THE FAMOUS WOMEN to whom Nostradamus paid particular attention in his prophecies. Others, such as Mary Queen of Scots, Elizabeth I of England, and Marie Antoinette, were given as much attention, and Nostradamus was also highly influenced by two other women during his life—his first wife, whose name we do not know, who died of the bubonic plague, and his second wife, Anne Ponsarde Gemelle, with whom he lived until his death. The deaths of his first wife and children are said by many who have studied his life to have been the catalyst for the beginning of his life's work as prophet. We can see from his prophecies that he was very aware of how female personal power and the tragedy of loss could alter male perspective, and his verses contain some very intimate details from what must have been intense experiences during his years of family life.

Nostradamus was both sensitive to the truths and the wisdom of life and deeply religious by nature. His understanding of and belief in godliness can be summed up by a line from his favorite philosopher, the medieval German mystic Meister Eckhart:

The eye, with which I see God sees me; my eye and God's eye is one eye, one seeing, one realizing and one love.

He could never be seen as a devout Catholic, for by heritage he was a Jew, his family having converted to the Catholic faith only to avoid the sanctions of the State. His great passion for the occult and alchemical beliefs of the time brought him a broader and far more intense view of religion than could have been provided by the bigotry of sixteenth-century religious leaders, and we can see this greater wisdom—evidence of his being a man greater than his own times—in almost all the attitudes he adopts towards the events that were to unfold before his eyes.

Below: Nostradamus, inside a magic circle, predicting the fate of future kings of France to Catherine de' Medici. From *La Nature*, Paris, 1887.

Previous pages:
Page 22: Ceration, "the mollification of a hard thing." This is the alchemical process—at once spiritual and chemical—by which matter is brought into a wax-like, soft or fluid state. From a sixteenth-century copy of Sir George Ripley's *The Compound of Alchymie Conteining Twelve Gates*, 1475, in the Bodleian Library, Oxford.

Page 23: Marie Antoinette, the ill-fated queen of Louis XVI of France.

Nostradamus used a number of methods to augment his gifts as a visionary, most of them profoundly magical or metaphysical in nature. He had a considerable knowledge of the great magicians of his own past, including that written down in several major works of the occult, which he either owned or had access to—books such as the _De Mysteriis Aegyptorum,_ a study of Chaldean and Assyrian magic written by Iamblichus, a fourth-century neo-Platonist of the Syrian school. Such volumes, it should be remembered, were regarded by the Church as highly heretical, and even owning a copy would probably have been sufficient to bring about a sentence of death through suspicion of black magic arts. Iamblichus' book certainly taught the black arts. Nostradamus also owned a manuscript called _De Daemonibus,_ a distinctly dark rendering of diabolic powers, written by the Byzantine philosopher and statesman Michael Psellus.

During one of the periods when he was at the greatest risk of being persecuted by the Church authorities Nostradamus burned a number of occult books, writing in his journals that they would have certainly misinterpreted their contents.

Much of his time was spent in the top floor garret of his house in Salon—a house which has now been turned into a museum. He would select astrologically propitious nights, suitable for the trance states that he would enter to find the visions of the future. Using either the flame of a single candle or water to gaze into, Nostradamus would perform rituals such as that proposed by the prophet Branchus from ancient Greece. This involved sitting on a brass tripod with the back upright, adopting an uncomfortable position so as to retain full awareness. The tripod was positioned so that the legs were at the same angle as the corners of the pyramids, thus encouraging what we know today to be an electro-magnetic field. This he believed would help concentrate the energies at his disposal. A brass bowl filled with hot water, various oils, and herbs with special powers, would stand before him. Finally, he would chant occult incantations to further enhance the whole process.

I emptied my soul, brain and heart of all care and attained a state of tranquillity and stillness of mind which are prerequisites for predicting by means of the brass tripod . . . human understanding being created by intellect cannot see secret things unless helped by voices from a void which is helped in turn by the thin candle flame...from which comes a clouded vision of great events, unhappy and important, cataclysmic adventures arriving in the right time.

PREFACE TO HIS SON CÉSAR

NOSTRADAMUS THE ASTROLOGER

STROLOGY is the study of the motion and relative positions of the planets, Sun, Moon and stars, in the belief that these movements can influence people's lives and show what will happen in the future. It embraces the principle that human beings and their environment are affected by their more remote surroundings. The planets are, after all, in touch with us, inasmuch as they surround us, draw upon our world gravitationally, and have remained in our orbit or each other's conjoined orbits from the very beginning of life on Earth.

For thousands of years before Nostradamus' time, the study of astrology was of the greatest importance to almost all civilizations, including the Greeks, the Egyptians and most of pagan Europe. The calculations of the positions of the known planets were precisely detailed by Nostradamus in his own ephemeris, and his calculations even seem to anticipate Newton's laws of gravity a century before they were proposed.

Nostradamus calculated elliptical orbits in his horoscopes well before they were written down by Johannes Kepler. We even find Kepler's horoscope amongst the workings that the Prophet undertook, and Kepler was born five years after Nostradamus had died!

Nostradamus also used astrological horoscopes to estimate the best timing of his treatments before administering them, so that the right moment would always be chosen, causing everything to remain in harmony. Harmony was of the essence in everything this remarkable prophet did.

Almost all the events that Nostradamus predicted have an astrological element to them, with the verses containing many references to the positions of planets, the Sun and the Moon in the heavens. His trance states and his occult gazing were almost invariably backed up by the use of astrological workings, with use of the cyclic nature of the heavens to date his predictions. We are given frequent hints within the quatrains as to the timing of an event, by references to the positions of planets and their conjunctions with one another. Although it is mostly the case that these cyclic conjunctions of the planets are repeated each century, or even each year, read together with other clues that the Prophet provides in his verses, we are able to get a fairly accurate dating for many of the predictions. Reading Nostradamus' words is therefore a little like a detective hunt.

Below: Many of Nostradamus' predictions were grounded in a thorough knowledge of astronomy and astrology. This fifteenth-century Flemish tapestry from Toledo Cathedral depicts an astrolabe and zodiac.

EMERGING FROM THE PATRIARCHAL SOCIETY

N EXAMINING NOSTRADAMUS' VERSES a picture emerges of how the increasing presence of women in positions of power begins to effect major changes in the balance of world events, altering the way in which global national relationships develop, and therefore also the way in which global finance matures into a more cooperative science. In the current patriarchal social order we have so internalized the "rules" imposed upon us, men and women alike, by thousands of years of male domination, that we cannot easily make conscious changes. It is as though we have become hypnotized by patriarchal concepts— as though they have become part of our very blood.

Right: Two prominent female figures of the recent past: Indira Gandhi, Prime Minister of India, and Jackie Kennedy, a symbol of woman's lack of power in the West.

Opposite: A carved figure from Benin, in West Africa, depicting the magical power of womanhood.

Even if we decide that patriarchal values are self-destructive, and must be changed, we find ourselves blocked. The institutions of any society function almost automatically to maintain that society as it is; and the ideology of any society functions to justify that status quo as being both necessary and beneficial. In capitalist and socialist states alike, enormous sums of money and great numbers of people are dependent upon the production of weapons. In each kind of state this situation is 'justified' by ideology that emphasizes the threat posed by the other kind of state; the moral argument is that amassing arms is necessary to protect a beneficial way of life. The ideology heightens the sense of conflict and fear, which in turn stimulates greater emphasis on defense, offense, and weaponry. The vicious cycle guarantees its own continuation . . . .

Marilyn French, Beyond Power

Right: New York power station, a symbol of man's ability to destroy his environment in the name of commerce.

Opposite: Celebrating midsummer's eve around the maypole in Sweden, where the ancient, female rights of pagan fertility are still celebrated.

As we shall see in Nostradamus' commentaries, the civilized world of the twentieth century has, in effect, built a rod for its own back, containing an intrinsic misery that is not present in primitive societies. Those who have lived with so-called "primitive" people over long periods of time have reported greater joy, longer life, more intense pleasure, greater health and a plethora of the more positive aspects of being alive.

In "civilized" patriarchal society we value sophistication, high-powered technology, material comforts and the power of thought. In primitive societies the emphasis is on feeling, being and relating and the net result is a sense of well-being and importance to the society—in contrast to the ever-present call of civilized society, where the average individual feels unnecessary, a "small cog in a big machine," and lacks a sense of self-worth.

Another of the prizes which civilized society has demanded, and on which it is possible to see Nostradamus commenting in his prophecies, is that of distraction. We work hard, carry a lot of stress, sleep badly, suffer anxiety in our efforts to increase our lot, and as a result need distractions such as fashion, games, movies and other entertainments which help us to move away from the humdrum, miserable reality we encounter on a daily basis. We thus enter a symbolic realm, which has already reached an ultimate state called "Virtual Reality," where it is possible almost literally to depart the here-and-now and enter the there-and-then—a final alienation from ourselves.

As part of this need for distraction we also want the methods by which we are distracted to be convenient. One of the main forces behind modern technology is

the provision of convenient methods of movement and activity in general. We don't have to walk for miles to wash our clothes, we don't have to spend months to get from one spot on the globe to another, like Nostradamus did in his arduous journey to Paris. We can use the washing machine in our own private laundry, we can take a car or a plane and be there in an hour. We have water on tap. Nobody would deny that these things are good in many ways, but in these technological advances we have also lost something along the way.

The inconveniences of these conveniences are hugely more complex and anxiety-ridden than the inconveniences they have replaced. Simply entering an airport is an increasingly unpleasant experience, and the traffic jams that get us there (or rather don't get us there) are perhaps eventually going to grow to a level where it will be necessary to walk across the rows of stationary vehicles that have been left on the highways by frustrated drivers. The noise level of city life has reached exhausting heights, while the pollution of the atmosphere is an escalating disaster from which we may never recover. This is to say nothing of the continuing little niggling worries that hound us all on a daily, even hourly, basis because of our need to keep up the payments on our conveniences so that we may drive to work amidst a steaming, angry, polluted environment. This is the technically proficient, overproductive consumer society that competitive patriarchal values have produced.

The most interesting and exciting aspect of Nostradamus' prophecies concerning the advent of a new social order is that the different "energy" of

Opposite: The price of plenty Chimney
stacks of industrial plant emitting smoke.

womankind appears to impinge on different aspects of life; the very reduction of the "male-method," according to this interpretation, provides a solution to our present impasse and a new paradigm for all areas of life. It is not simply that we see a change from patriarchal to matriarchal values, but a change in the balance of power, so to speak, which brings about a completely new vision of how life can function. This vision applies in the broadest of spectrums, affecting life at its foundations, for example changing the whole concept of hierarchy, which in turn impacts on the social and political aspects of life.

The prophecies also touch upon certain discoveries in medical science concerning the way the body heals itself through formerly misunderstood natural cycles, and how the balance of hormones in women connects with the Earth's rhythms. It appears that men will learn to harness the magic of female energy as a cure for many of the sicknesses that are defying medicine during the late twentieth century, and that this "female learning" in men will also alter the economic concepts of capitalism, and the ever-present hunt for the "fast buck."

With the increase in authority of women, we will also see a growth in the importance of magic and instinct over science and rational thinking. In fact, if we take what Nostradamus has to say at all seriously, the movement of women into positions of greater power and equality, and the resulting change from the prevailing patriarchal values in the civilized world to something more feminine and instinctual, may well be the only hope humanity has for survival.

WOMEN
AS LAW

THE BEGINNING OF THE TRANSFORMATION

ONE OF THE MOST NOTABLE FEATURES of Nostradamus' time was the exclusively autocratic hierarchical political and religious structure within Europe, "the great chain of being" on Earth reflecting exactly the view of the divine subscribed to by the Church and State. The old elective kingships of tribal and medieval Europe had long given way to absolute monarchies established by heredity. Succession to the throne was determined by right of primogeniture and consecrated by the Church—the king was "the Lord's anointed." Autocratic rule was thus based upon a partnership between Church and State, with the divine right of kings to govern entrenched in popular belief.

The process was totally male, with God "the Father" handing down his power to the sovereign, who then placed power in the hands of lords, lesser barons, and so on. The father in the home was finally the lord and master of his mini-realm, and so the male-dominated social structure flourished. The very few female sovereigns of the day managed to rule through considerable strength and determination, but were actually regarded by society as masculine. The reign of a queen such as Elizabeth I did not produce a matriarchal structure within any social environment, neither in government nor within the family unit. Nor did it produce a balance of power between men and women, or any special form of co-operation or harmony greater than had existed with a king. Men were still in charge, which seemed the natural order of things.

The biblical and popular image of God as a great patriarch in heaven, rewarding and punishing humanity according to his mysterious ways, has dominated the imagination of the Judeo-Christian community for two thousand years. The image of a male "God the Father," first born as a symbol in a patriarchal society and then sustained as plausible by patriarchy until today, has meant that the hierarchical order of both Heaven and Earth were aligned according to an exclusively male order.

If God in *his* heaven is a father ruling *his* people, then it is according to *his* divine plan that society on earth be male-dominated.

The mystical relationships between humanity and God, between men and women, reflected this lop-sided concept. The images, symbols, and values of this belief system were sustained in Judeo-Christian religion, becoming fixed as "Articles of Faith." In this context, the oppression of women appeared only right and fitting.

The vicious cycle was further exacerbated by the fact that the roles, structures, beliefs, and symbols of

Vnitas simpl...
Principium.
Terminus a...
Fons essentia...
Actus primu...
Ens entium...
.Natura natur...

DEVS

Mens.
2. Seraphin.
3. Cherubin.
4. Dominationes.
5. Throni.
6. Potestates.
7. Principatus.
8. Virtutes.
9. Archangeli.
10. Angeli.
11. Cælum Stellatum.
12. Saturnus.
13. Iupiter.
14. Mars.
15. Sol.
16. Venus.
17. Mercuri.
18. Luna.
19. Ignis.
20. Aer.
21. Aqua.
22. Terra.

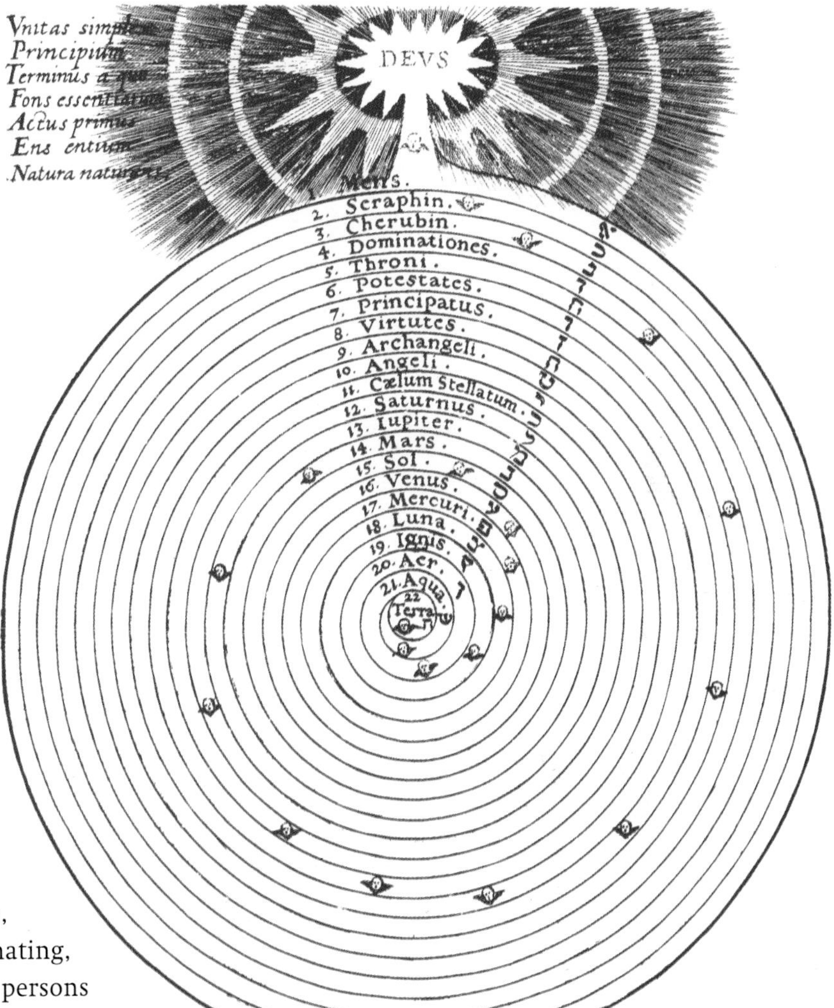

this patriarchal society were developed according to an artificial polarization of human qualities into the traditional sexual stereotypes. The masculine universe was seen as objective, aggressive, hyper-rational, dominating, manipulating nature and other persons (namely women). The feminine universe was stereotyped as being hyper-emotional, passive, and self-abnegating. In this unbalanced view the masculine was safely constant and unchanging; the feminine was mutant and changing, dangerously unpredictable. The universe and its reflection, the world and its inhabitants, were unwisely divided between Male and Female.

This sex-role segregation of women, which kept them locked in a symbolic ghetto for centuries, was the first stone laid to pave the road to the history of antifeminism. Patriarchal religion first invented and then sustained the dynamics of delusion of such a universe,

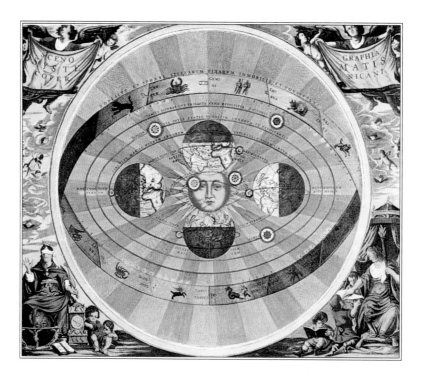

naming them as "natural," reflective of a divine order, and bestowing supernatural blessings upon them.

There was thus a clear difference between what was "corruptible"—that is, changeable and therefore feminine—and what was eternal or fixed, and therefore masculine. This fundamental philosophy produced anger and contempt for the world, for the distinction between male and female was the distinction between staying the same and changing.

In Nostradamus' time, and still today, the Moon represented the inconstant (or mutable) as opposed to the fixed and eternal. Anything born under the full Moon, or susceptible to the influence of lunar forces (such as witchcraft or the menstrual cycle) was viewed as suspect. Everything that was removed from lunar influence—such as the Earth (which was seen as the center of the universe), heaven, God—that did not change, was good. Matter, flesh—particularly of the female variety—was corruptible, while the soul was eternal. Therefore the body was seen as contemptible while the soul, regarded as masculine, rose after death (the only time of joy) to join God. No wonder then that Church fathers like Tertullion declared that women "are the devil's gateway," or that Thomas Aquinas defined women as "misbegotten males."

This conceptual framework formed the basis of male domination, because the center—the soul, God, good—was the power around which everything else—the body, mutability, femininity—orbited. Obedience was therefore essential, and the orbiting body of woman had to obey the central power—man. This was, and still is, men as law.

Patriarchy sustained a view of the universe which was self-reflective, thus unchangeable, static. For anyone to hint that this was not so, that the universe had what were erroneously believed to be "feminine" qualities—that is, that it was mutable and changeable—meant a deviation from the status-quo belief system. Any such statements and theories were thus deemed blasphemous.

But at about the time of Nostradamus, there lived another astronomer and physician who would become a major influence on European thought, whose ideas encapsulated the New Learning of the Renaissance, and who would open the way to the power of change and the new feminine spirit. His name was Nicholas Copernicus.

Copernicus, a Polish astronomer, proposed that the Earth rotated daily on its axis and orbited the Sun, and not vice versa. This meant that the Earth was nothing more than one of several planets traveling around the Sun, which was the center of the known universe. Copernicus also stated that the universe in fact went far further than the local system and was, as far as could be divined, infinite. Because of the controversial nature of his findings, his treatise was not published until the year of his death, 1543.

Others then took up this concept and happily developed it, some to their fatal disadvantage. The heretical philosopher Giordano Bruno was burned at the stake for suggesting that the universe was mutable—subject to change, and therefore feminine in nature. Other astronomers suggested that the orbits of the planets were elliptical and not perfect circles—in other words not the holy, perfect symmetry that the Church had, in its ignorance, positively asserted. Galileo even suggested that the light of the Moon was a reflection of the Sun's rays and that the Sun also moved in an orbit, rather than remaining fixed in one, eternal place.

All this caused no end of embarrassment to the established Church, for it suggested that perhaps the patriarchal model was faulty, to say the least.

Using his powers of divination, his knowledge of astrology based upon the Copernican view of the universe, and ancient alchemical and occult devices, Nostradamus made his own mark on the growing, more open-minded view of the universe. His

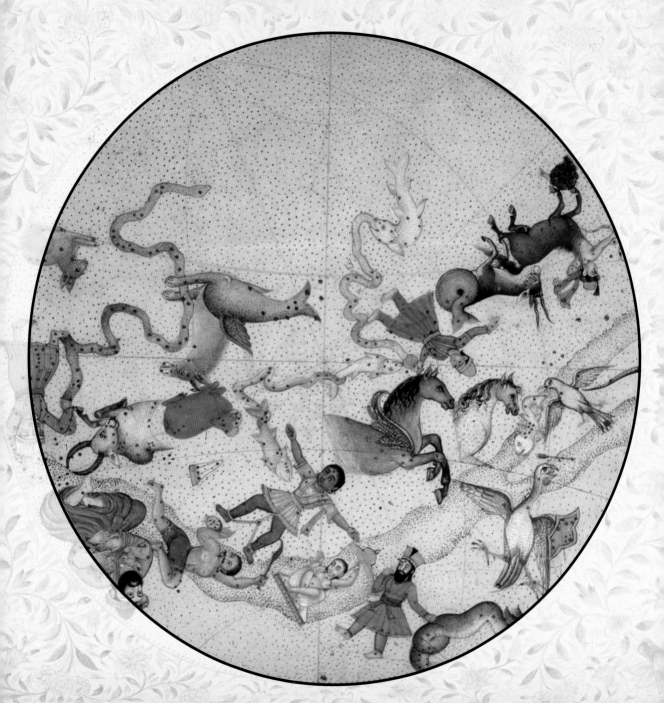

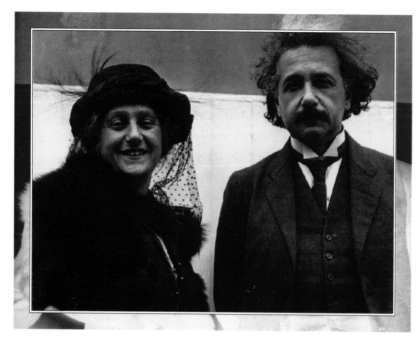

Left: "Dr. Albert Einstein and his wife," reads the caption for this photograph. No mention of Mrs. Einstein's name is given!

Opposite: The Shri yantra—the most powerful of the Tantric yantras, or diagrams to meditate upon—is at once active and essentially feminine. The Indian cult of Tantra focuses on the female as the most direct approach to the intuition of the truth.

Previous pages: A Sanskrit manuscript star map, showing the Eastern and Western hemispheres with constellations. British Library, London.

writings about the future, as we shall see, contain a number of predictions concerning women and their coming powers.

The male, patriarchal world view was essentially mechanistic in outlook, and continued to remain strong, particularly with the development of classical physics in the Western scientific tradition.

Isaac Newton's universal law of gravitation posited an absolute framework within which forces of attraction acted between separate, rigidly connected bodies. Thus, a force of gravity coming from the Sun acted upon the planets, determining their orbits. After overcoming its resistance to the idea of a helio-centric universe, the Church found comfort in the fixed rigidity of this theory, as it supported a patriar-chal view of immutability. But, in our own century, scientists such as Einstein and his contemporaries examining the conundrum of quantum mechanics—

people like Schroedinger and others—shattered this certainty and brought into play far more complex and "doubtful" theories relating to the absolute and constant presence of the inabsolute and inconstant. They proposed such unlikely and "unpatriarchal" concepts as the fact that subatomic particles can be both waves and particles simultane-ously, that they can be both indestructible and destructible, that mass varies with velocity, that mass and energy distort space and time, and that time and space are actually connected!

It has even been suggested, via concepts such as Schroedinger's Cat in the Box paradox, that the very existence of life is no more than the extended vision of human thought patterns, and without the existence of our eyes and our brains, none of this would exist at all! What does this do to the patriar-chal need for fixed certainties?

Gazing into his steaming hot, magical, changing, divining bowl, Nostradamus foresaw the end of arid male rationalism.

THE NEW BALANCE
OF THE FEMININE

New law to occupy the new land
Towards Syria, Judea and Palestine:
The great barbarian empire of men to decay,
Before the Moon completes its cycle.
CENTURY 3:97

A new law will emerge in the new world of America, at
a time when Syria, Judea and Palestine are significant:
the great barbarian empire of patriarchy that men
have created will decay during the time that the
feminine spirit is completing its cycle.

ONE OF THE MOST PERVASIVE CHARACTERISTICS of the
patriarchal status quo is its dependence on
division, on the differences between things
as opposed to the similarities they share. Where
differences arise, so superiorities and inferiorities are
born. The whole basis of this concept of duality—right
and wrong, black and white, good and bad, man or
woman—is male in origin and naturally gives rise to
the corollary of one being either legally or morally
better than the other. There are even remaining
associations in the twentieth century which perpetuate the distinctions, for example between left and
right. This state of opposites can be seen in such
bizarre differences as the way we button our shirts!
Men's shirts button on the right, women's on the left.
At a wedding ceremony the groom's party sits on the

47

right and the bride's on the left. This custom derives from what we now call superstitions from the past, but which at the time of their inception were considered seriously, even medically, and certainly religiously, as facts of life. Jesus sat on the right hand of God, and during banquets and feasts, even everyday meals, the favored child, probably the son, or a good friend, would sit on the right side of the "man of the house." The devil always stands on the left shoulder of the unfortunate sinner, which is why we throw salt over the left shoulder to blind him. We mostly write with the right hand, not the left, and left-handed people tend to be thought of as a little different, or perhaps eccentric. In medical science, during very early parts of this century, it was believed that semen from the right testicle produced boys and that from the left, girls. It is notable that the part of the woman in this "decision" was seemingly not relevant. Men determined everything.

However, when it comes to the brain, matters concerned with left and right go sadly wrong. The left side of the brain, according to modern medicine, performs the logical, ordered and linear functions of our lives, while the right has a holistic point of view and performs activities requiring intuition, creativity and visualization. And the "crowning" discovery is that the best results are achieved from learning to co-ordinate the sides equally so that a balance is found in our daily lives. Modern psychology and particularly the "new age" philosophies derived from a greater exposure to Eastern, especially Indian, concepts, preach the basic necessity of integration, of bringing the male and female within each of us to bear on all life's demands. But first, according to Nostradamus, the feminine must reach a higher peak of power.

With a view to exploring this progress we begin with the verse quoted at the beginning of this section, in

which Nostradamus' words tell us much more than at first appears.

A new law will emerge in the new world of America,
at a time when Syria, Judea and Palestine
are significant:
the great barbarian empire of patriarchy that men
have created will decay during the time that the
feminine spirit is completing its cycle.

He expresses his meaning through extremely economical language, as we can see if we look at the original verse at the beginning of this section. The first line directs us to the location of this new law. To sixteenth-century Europeans, the mythical attributes and untapped potential of the New World were a powerful magnet. Throughout his verses Nostradamus frequently refers to "the new land" to mean America. This is an established interpretation, and in this case the "new law" which will arise there is related, in the last two lines, to two factors—the existence of a "barbarian" male empire, which is in decay, which is in turn related to the Moon and its cycles—a common metaphorical association with woman. Put simply, the great virgin territories of the New World will be the source of a rising "lunar" consciousness at a time when the Judeo-Christian

Right: Women join the ranks of the judiciary in Great Britain.

tradition is at its peak—the brute rule of patriarchy will start to crumble before the female evolution is complete. This is the beginning of our story, and the position that humanity has reached at the end of the twentieth century.

Nostradamus foresaw democracy as a force in human affairs which would supersede the autocratic monarchies of his day. These, he predicted, would thus be gradually replaced or replenished by a greater female influence, producing in its turn an entirely new world order. This process is the fundamental theme of the book, as we see the prediction of the accretion of a "critical mass" of feminine power unfold within the prophet's verses.

As an underlying feature of women's position in society, and as a part of Nostradamus' predicted "new law," which we can take quite literally as referring to the legal aspects of society, we shall see changes, for example, in institutions such as the criminal and civil justice systems of the United States and European countries; these will facilitate greater female equality and give women an increasingly important position during the last years of this millennium and the first decade of the next.

In order for women to be able to function, independently of male influence, it has already, during the first half of the 1990s, become apparent that in the established judicial processes with regard to women's

Opposite: Pallas Athene, by Gustav Klimt, 1898. In antiquity the Goddess Athena represented moral integrity, psychological insight and practical wisdom. She was often portrayed with an owl.

rights there are major holes which need to be blocked. Areas of criminal and civil law such as those governing rape, sexual abuse and marital abuse are the subject of heated debate, and there have been more court cases surrounding these aspects of the law in the early 1990s than ever before in history. Within the more militant sectors of the women's liberation movement there is a sense of anger against "sexist" institutions, particularly in America, where attitudes against male domination are growing stronger every year.

Male-dominated institutions from the political arena all the way to the Roman Catholic Church are finding themselves under attack, and there has already been a considerable growth of female power in many sectors. According to the book *Megatrends For Women* by Patricia Aburdene and John Naisbitt:

- In 1993, 38 per cent of the House of Representatives legislature in Washington were women.
- In the United States there were, in 1993, more than five million female-owned businesses which contributed more jobs than the whole of the Fortune 500 companies put together.

One of the most important messages within the quatrains is that there will come a time, close to the end of this millennium, when a critical mass of female power will occur. The timing of this change is established by the fact that Nostradamus makes frequent reference to the "new world" or "new country," meaning America, as being the catalyst for such change. The United States has become a Super Power only in the last half of this century.

The concept of "critical mass" was formulated first in physics which defined it as the minimum quantity of radioactive material needed to produce a nuclear chain reaction. In human terms, a critical mass may occur in a social environment where dissatisfaction grows to a level where revolution occurs, simply through the gathering of enough angry people in one place, all with sufficient energy to force change. The surrounding environmental and social response to this catalyst also plays a part in the size and shape of the resulting new paradigm. Once this critical mass has reached its peak, the result is a self-sustaining change. Paradigm shifts occur in this way. As we shall see in this chapter, Nostradamus' verses can be interpreted to predict the formation of a critical mass of women with a militant march across Europe.

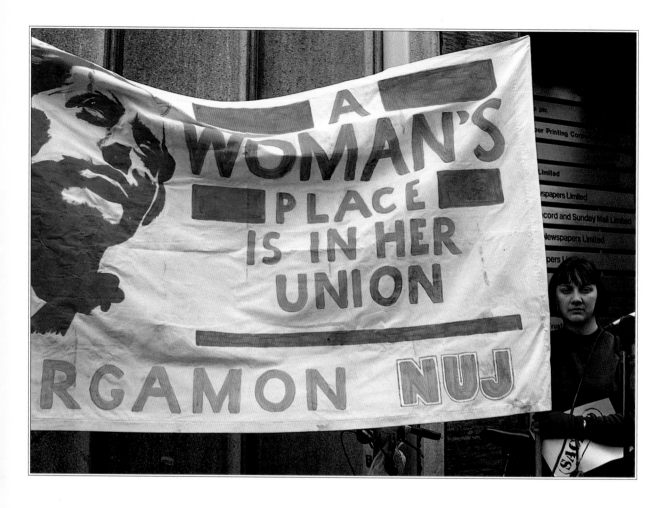

THE SELINE MOVEMENT

CCORDING TO THE VERSES QUOTED BELOW, a large group of women will take a militant stand in order to effect major changes within contemporary society. We may feel that this has already happened during the 1980s and early 1990s, with militant feminism playing a strong part in helping to shift the stubborn male domain, but according to this interpretation of Nostradamus there is more to come, for in truth the patriarchal format still dominates the civilized world. First come the literal translations of the verses, and then there follows a more free interpretation.

Opposite: A banner at a union march in the United Kingdom symbolizes the beginning of female power in the workplace.

From the shore of Lake Garda to Lake Fucino,
Taken from the Lake of Geneva to the port of "L'Orguion:"
Born of three arms the predicted warlike image,
Through three crowns to great Endymion.

From Sens, from Autun they will come as far as the Rhone
To pass beyond and towards the Pyrenees mountains:
The nation to leave the march at Ancona:
By land and sea it will be followed by great trails.

The voice of the unusual bird is heard
On the pipe (or canon) of the floor
So high will come from the wheat the bushel
That man will be a cannibal to man.

Lightning in Burgundy will make something portentous,
One which could never have happened through skill,
A sexton made lame by the senate
Will inform the enemy of the matter.

Thrown back because of bows, fires, pitch and more fire:
Cries, shouts are heard at midnight:
Inside they are put onto broken battlements,
The traitors fled by underground passageways.

Great Neptune from the deep sea
With Punic forces mixed with Gallic blood.
The Isles bleed, because of the late rowing:
More harm will it do to him, the badly conceived secret.

The beard sizzled and black because of skill
Will reduce the cruel and proud people:
The great Chyren will remove from far away
All those captured by the banner of Selin.

After the conflict by the eloquence of the one that is wounded
For a short while a false rest is managed:
The great ones are not to be allowed to be delivered at all
They are returned by the enemy at the right time.

Through fire from the sky the city is almost burned:
The Urn threatens Deucalion again:
Sardinia made angry by the Punic foist,
After Libra will leave her Phaethon.

Through hunger the prey will make the wolf prisoner,
The aggressor then in extreme distress.
The heir having the last one before him,
The great one does not escape in the middle of the crowd.

CENTURY 2:73-82

These are amongst the most fascinating of all the quatrains in the *Centuries,* particularly as they seem to form a story running longer than any other series of verses referring, or appearing to refer, to one event. It can be inferred from this that the event described—a march of women, under the *banner of Selin* (the Moon goddess Selene), across the power centers of Europe—is one of the most significant in history. And although during the late twentieth century some may not expect there to be a need for still greater feminine militancy, there is little doubt in the authors' minds that it is time that the patriarchal system fell by the wayside. Previous societies,

pre-Sumerian, pre-Egyptian, early European, have lived by different codes, without the domination, competitiveness and aggressiveness of the modern world, and they have been shown through recent anthropological discoveries to have lived more happily and with less misery than ourselves. As we shall see in the coming pages, Nostradamus foresaw a similar world to those ancient, peaceful, non-patriarchal societies, returning to Earth through the influence of woman.

So perhaps we can first "free-interpret" the lines of these verses to examine more closely where the prediction leads us.

From the shore of Lake Garda (in northeastern Italy) to the former Lake Fucino (now drained, an area of land sixty-five miles east of Rome) moving from Lake Geneva (in Switzerland) to the port of the Orgueil (to be discussed later) born out of three labors according to a predicted warlike image through three wreaths to the great lover of the Moon (Endymion, son of Zeus, was the lover of Selene, goddess of the Moon).

From Sens (northeast France, then in the Duchy of Burgundy) and Autun (also in Burgundy, one hundred miles from Sens) they will come as far as from the River Rhone to travel as far as the Pyrenees mountains, of those arising in Italy, a group of people will leave the march at Ancona (east coast of Italy); by land and sea it will be followed by great trails.

A big, unusual bird (possibly a bird of prey or a symbol) will be high in the sky where the air is still breathable; down near the earth is a layer that is not breathable, where men live and a famine exists, making men cannibals.

Powers in Burgundy will inflict punishment on the people of the march, and this will be told to the marchers by a disempowered cleric serving the State. They will be repelled by fire and weapons with cries heard at midnight and traitors to the cause will escape through underground passages.

Forces (probably military or police) from the Ottoman Empire and France (a fundamentalist backlash) will stand against the march, coming from the sea, though because of a late start will fail to stop it.

Men (bearded), burned by the skill of the marchers, will fight and beat them cruelly. The great comet Chiron will be seen moving far away by all those under the banner of Seline.

After the conflict an eloquent individual who was wounded secures a truce, which proves to be false, for the rest of the marchers, while those leaders who were captured by the enemy (presumably men) are returned at the right time.

Because of bombs or rockets a city nearby is burned: the son of the creator of mankind (Deucalion was the son of Prometheus, the creator of mankind in Greek mythology, whose task it was to renew the human race) is threatened again and the conflict is made worse by involvement from the people of Sardinia, which, after Libra (an astrological reference) will leave her Phaethon (a mythological reference to be explained).

Because of a yearning the women will make the men prisoners, so that they are very distressed. Even if the new heir (woman) stands behind the great one (man), she will now be noticed.

Right: Rally in Boston for federal funding for breast cancer research and education. Women increasingly are taking the initiative on issues that concern them.

In translating and interpreting these complex and fascinating lines, we have used a number of devices.

- Local historical references and symbols that have some connection with the lifetime and locations of Nostradamus himself. In the authors' previous book—*Nostradamus: The Millennium and Beyond*—it was suggested that Nostradamus used his own period of history, including people and locations, as metaphors for events in the future.

- Mythological symbolism from the distant past— such as Greek mythological heroes like Phaethon.

- A knowledge of history as it has developed up to the twentieth century—in other words, we are aware that there is a growing feminine movement, and have therefore applied this knowledge to the verses.

Employing the above methods the outlines of a story are revealed, of a march of women across Europe involving a large part of Italy, Switzerland and France, initially to establish rights that have not been granted to them, but evolving into a very significant event on the global scene. These rights may well concern equality, money and effectiveness in society, and by the tone of the overall prediction, this is a major event also in the history of womankind. The march undertaken, presumably, by a large

Opposite: The route of the Seline March, expected, according to this interpretation of Nostradamus, to take place in the late twentieth century.

number of women, derives from a number of starting points: northern Italy, the area of Rome, from Switzerland near Lake Geneva, and an area which is given the title "L'Orguion" which is interpreted by Edgar Leoni (one of the most prosaic and intelligent interpreters of Nostradamus) to refer to the town of Orgon, twenty miles north of Salon, where Nostradamus lived, and which was, perhaps either coincidentally or significantly, an area where in 1864 a meteorite fell. This meteorite was found to contain elements of carbon, seeds, reed and other fragments, indicating the presence of life in another part of the universe. On closer examination it became clear that these items had been embedded there deliberately, in an attempt to create a hoax. This reference may have some significance once the march of the Seline Movement occurs.

Something that needs to be understood about Nostradamus' visions is that very often scenes and concepts, words and facts might be given to him which made little sense even to him, so that we are interpreting something which can only ultimately be verified when and if it actually occurs.

In the free interpretation we see that the movement is born out of three labors and a "predicted warlike image" of three wreaths, under the lovers of Endymion, whom we connect through mythology with the Moon. It is said that Nostradamus himself was unable to interpret this enigmatic verse, though there are those in his future (the interpreter Allen, who wrote in 1943) who believe it refers to America because of the mythological connection between Endymion and Selene, who put him into a perpetual slumber so that she could caress him at will. Why this should be seen as a metaphor for the United States is something of a mystery, unless we believe that in the context of feminism, the United States is asleep to the feminine spirit, or else that man has put woman to sleep so that he may caress her without ever waking her.

A more likely explanation is that the banner carried by the women of the Seline Movement contains

Opposite: *Opposite:* The return of Halley's Comet in 1910. Because of the regular nature of their orbits, comets were a popular device in Nostradamus' prophetic timing. At one point in the march of the Seline Movement, there is said to be sight of a comet in the sky.

symbols of labor and three victors' wreaths that have some significance at the time, and this warlike image associated with the Moon is clearly another symbolic reference to the need for an aggressive and powerful stance by women to achieve their ends. The Moon as symbol of womanhood is clear.

The story continues, telling us which regions the marchers will come from and where they will all march to—converging, it seems, on Ancona, on the eastern coast of Italy.

We then read of conditions which sound extreme, to say the least. High in the sky the air is breathable, whereas close to the ground the atmosphere is polluted and men suffer from famine (in the original, Nostradamus refers to the pipe of the air-vent floor, an extraordinary piece of twentieth-century description for a sixteenth-century writer). Nostradamus has a habit of expressing things in an extreme way, but if we consider how our own time would have looked from his vantage point—before the industrial revolution, when air was pure, when motor vehicles were unknown and rivers and oceans were still free from pollution—it might well seem to him that our air was not breathable, and that we were suffering from famine. It could also be that he was not necessarily referring to famine in Italy, but in other parts of the world, thus giving us a time frame to date the prediction.

In effect, this Seline Movement, and the march across Europe, are linked to the modern industrial age and could therefore occur at any time in the latter years of this century.

We then receive some details of hostile local governments (the Burgundians, in the previous century, had captured Joan of Arc and handed her over to the English for trial) and of escapes through underground passages, together with political and military forces (*Punic forces mixed with Gallic blood*, that is both Christian and Islamic) being deployed to prevent the march from progressing.

This march will, incidentally, be the first to occur across several borders, a truly international revolutionary march. Its route, perhaps coincidentally, according to Nostradamus' description, traces in reverse Hannibal's march against Rome in 218 B.C. during the Second Punic War—traveling over the Alps, down the Rhone Valley into southern France and then to Spain—somehow signifying a reversal of historical process. The journey from Rome to Carthage can be seen as a return to the early Mediterranean religion.

In the sky, during the march of the Seline Movement, the comet Chiron will be seen passing overhead. Chiron is an old and regular "friend" of planet Earth. During the 1970s it was thought to be another planet moving in an unstable orbit between Saturn and

Uranus, but after a dust envelope was detected around its orbit in the 1980s it was re-classified as a comet.

Nostradamus is very keen on comets, which crop up frequently in his predictions. Because of their cyclic nature, they are a useful device for timing events in the future. Why he should have chosen Chiron to be the comet seen by the women of the Seline Movement is a mystery, because it is not generally visible in the night sky without the help of a powerful telescope; so there may be another reason for this reference. It could be that he was telling us to look both at the comet Chiron and at the mythological associations of its name, in order to give some idea of when this event will take place. We discover, if we look into Greek mythology, that Chiron was a wise Centaur who, after being wounded, was transformed by the gods into the constellation Sagittarius, which lies between Scorpio and Capricorn in the Zodiac. The Sun passes through Sagittarius from November to December, up to the winter solstice (December 21/22), so we can infer that the march will take place at this time of the year. Unfortunately Chiron, in the course of its solar orbit, is only occasionally visible on Earth, when it happens to be lit by the Sun's rays, and we cannot therefore predict a year when this might occur.

The story continues with details of a deal made by one who is wounded and eloquent, which fails, but

Left: The Scales—symbol of the astrological sign of Libra.

Opposite: A protester against the Catholic Church's narrowly defined morality.

which results in the return of prisoners.

The conflict created by these marchers appears to be on a large scale, for we are next informed of bombs, rockets and a burned city, with involvement by the people of the island of Sardinia, provoked by *the Punic foist*—the spiritual return to Carthage.

Here we are given a typical Nostradamus reference, combining astrology and ancient mythology.

It takes the form of three separate, though connected references:

- Deucalion
- After Libra
- Phaethon

Deucalion, King of Phthia, was the son of Prometheus, the Titan who created human beings and gave them fire, in Greek mythology. Like Noah, Deucalion survived a Flood, let loose by Zeus, in an ark—a moonship, in the Mesopotamian version. His task was to renew the human race after its fall, an important metaphor, for Nostradamus sees the evolution of woman as being highly significant in the rebirth of humanity.

The reference to *after Libra* indicates both a planetary movement and a metaphorical reference to justice. Libra represents the scales of justice, perhaps giving us another indication of the Prophet's view of woman's ideal place in the balance of society. In astrological terms it lies between Virgo and Scorpio, and the Sun passes through Libra during October. *After Libra* takes us

Right: The alchemical mystery of "generation," from George Ripley's manuscript. Written in verse, this outlined the the twelve processes needed to develop the *magnum opus*, or Philosopher's Stone. Each of the twelve stages was linked to a sign of the zodiac.

Opposite: Bearing the US flag, Mrs. Herbert Carpenter marches for the Women's Suffrage Movement. An undated, hand-colored photograph from the last century.

Overleaf: Suffragette parade in New York City, May 1912.

to the December/January period in which the comet Chiron returns to our skies. It is as though we are receiving a detailed timeline of the progress of the march. We then learn of a connection with Phaethon.

Phaethon is the Greek word for shining, or radiant. In Greek mythology Phaethon was the son of the Sun god, Helios, and the nymph Rhode. Phaethon plagued his father to allow him to drive the chariot of the Sun through the heavens for a single day. His wish was granted, but Phaethon was unable to control the horses and the chariot traveled first so high that everyone shivered, and then so close to the Earth that he scorched it. To prevent severe damage Zeus struck him with a thunderbolt, causing him to fall into the Eridanus (Po) river. He was mourned by his sisters, Prote and Clymene, who turned into poplar trees on its banks, weeping amber tears.

The reference reiterates that the Sun is in the astrological house of Libra. The allegorical aspect of these words emphasizes that men will be brought low through their folly. All this apparently takes place in the months December/January of the year that Chiron becomes visible from Earth.

The last paragraph rounds off the story by telling us that whatever occurs in this mighty stand by women, the result will be an undeniable, greater presence of the feminine spirit in the world.

If we accept this interpretation of the verses, the march by a group called "Seline" is one of the pivotal features of women's evolution which will develop a militant format in the coming years and will push feminine power and equality further along the road, so forming the central core of the feminine critical mass.

We may presume this, then to be a very significant event in our future.

WOMEN
AT THE TOP

With a name so timid will she be brought forth
That the three sisters will have the name of destiny:
Then she will lead a great people by tongue and deed,
More than any other will she have fame and renown.

CENTURY 1:76

I IS PROPOSED THAT THIS QUATRAIN applies to the events resulting from the "revolt" on the part of women of the Seline Movement. A free interpretation of the verse follows:

The timid name of woman will be dispelled and she will be raised up to greater importance. The three sisters of womanhood (a classical reference to be explained) will find their place in destiny: then she will lead a great people by word and deed, and more than any other will she have fame and renown.

Put simply, womankind had, previous to the Seline

Movement, been associated with weakness, at least in the eyes of men. But not before time, she will be raised to much greater heights of importance. Here again we see the number three applied to the women's movement, a number previously encountered in the long story related to the Seline Movement, and which we shall see again when we look at how the future develops as a result of it. The three sisters in this case are allegorized from classical mythology and refer to the three ages of woman—virgin, mother and old woman. The "Triple Goddess" is referred to in *The Great Cosmic Mother* by Monica Sjöö and Barbara Mor.

75

Left: The three ages of woman.
Page 72: Pope John Paul II and
Queen Elizabeth II at
Buckingham Palace in 1982.

The moon, as daughter of the Great Mother, is known as the Triple Goddess. She presides over all acts of generation, whether physical, intellectual, or spiritual. Her triple aspect expresses the three phases of the moon: waxing (growth), full (rebirth) and waning (periodic death).

She is, as the New or Waxing Moon, the White Goddess of birth and growth.

She is, as the Full Moon, the Red Goddess of love and battle.

She is, as the Old or Waning Moon, the Black Goddess of death and divination.

These are the three phases of the womans life, all natural and all magical.

This reference helps us to understand the concept that Nostradamus was perhaps trying to portray in this verse—the renewed presence of woman as the center of magic in the world. The last line of the verse reaffirms that woman will play a much stronger part in leading the world and will enjoy great fame and fortune.

The first and most obvious areas in which this new power is likely to be felt are in the State and Church, and in his use of words such as "destiny" and "fame and renown" we can interpret Nostradamus as hinting at the increasing likelihood of women acceding to positions of power in government—women such as

Opposite: Women have begun, in the latter decades of the twentieth century, to enter all areas of business successfully, contributing ever more to the economic growth of the Western world.

Margaret Thatcher (who some interpreters believe will return to power in the late 1990s), Hillary Clinton, Ann Richards (until recently Governor of Texas), and Barbara Boxer (Californian Senator). This applies to women in other countries around the world—to Violeta Chamorro, who defeated Daniel Ortega to lead Nicaragua in 1990; in Brazil, to Luiza Erundina de Souza, currently mayor of São Paulo; in Japan, to Sadako Ogata, currently Japan's highest ranking official at the United Nations; in the Philippines, to Corazón Aquino; in Pakistan, to Benazir Bhutto, prime minister once again; in Russia, to Larisa Kuznetsova and Tatyana Ivanova, currently heads of the Moscow Women's Political Club. All these women are part of what will eventually be the norm throughout the world, the first step towards the critical mass of feminist political power. Then there is the presence of women in the established Churches, whom we will examine more closely later in the book.

One of the other areas that women will, of course, have an increasing impact on is in the business arena.

Figures quoted in *Megatrends for Women* by Patricia Aburdene and John Naisbitt show that during 1977 there were only 2 million female-owned businesses in the United States, turning over revenues of $25 billion. By 1988 there were 5 million female-owned businesses with revenues of over $83 billion. During that eleven-year period independent businesses overall increased revenues by some 56 per cent, while female businesses increased by over 129 per cent. According to figures published in various United States economic journals, this trend is continuing and increasing in a giant exponential curve towards the end of the millennium, contributing enormously to the general critical mass of the feminine spirit.

In order to establish a time-line for future predictions, it is necessary to place a date, even if it is slightly random, upon the start of what we would call the feminist movement. The most obvious era would be the 1960s, when women really began to stand up and be counted; but for that matter we could also date it much earlier, for during the first years of this century

Emily Pankhurst was responsible for winning women the vote, so perhaps this entire period of history right up to today should really be considered to be the prelude to the true feminine revolution. This view is certainly consistent with the predictions we are examining, and with the general interpretation of this book. For the sense of the prophecies is that women's liberation has really only just begun.

In *Megatrends for Women* Patricia Aburdene and John Naisbitt state:

This book takes women's liberation as a point of departure and asks, What comes next?

We therefore suggest that the real women's movement has only just begun in the early 1990s, and this will act as our point of departure for any dates and times given in Nostradamus' quatrains.

THE FAMILY OF WOMAN

The Moon hidden in deep shadows,
Her brother passes iron like,
The great one hidden for a long time under the eclipses,
Iron will cool in the bloody wound.

CENTURY 1: 84

TILL MORE FUNDAMENTAL TO THE FORTUNES OF WOMEN is their growing influence over love and the family. Though there has been, during the past few decades, a powerful swing of the pendulum towards feminism and a greater equality of the sexes, Nostradamus indicates that the years of determina- tion, culminating in a final militant mass march, result ultimately in female predominance both in the world at large and within the family at home.

In the quatrain at the beginning of this section we find a prediction related to the dwindling of male power—*Iron will cool*—at the hands of the female

wound. Nostradamus seems to be pointing to the likelihood of positive changes occurring once the concept of "feminine energy" becomes better understood in the hitherto male-dominated world—once the *banner of Selin* has been established following the march across Europe.

The result of our critical mass for change, however, is not simply the replacement of male dominance by female, but a completely new paradigm of men and women finding their full potential in co-operation with one another. During the latter years of the twentieth century the pendulum, presently moving away from the point in the arc that has kept men in power, swings more rapidly to the other side, where female power is felt more urgently. During the twenty-first century it settles near the center, finding a more co-operative and relaxed atmosphere between the sexes.

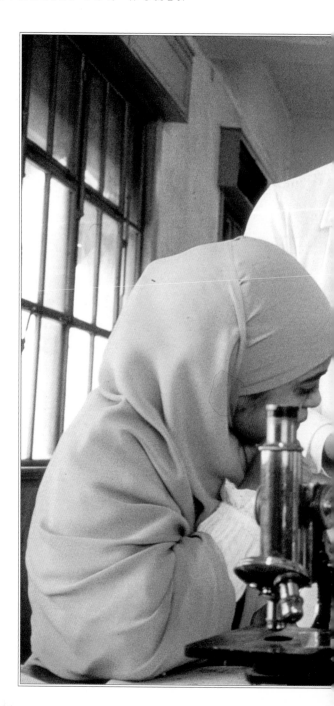

Right: Veiled medical students at Cairo University.

Previous pages:
Page 80: Annular eclipse at San Diego on January 4, 1992, during which the Moon passed directly in front of the setting Sun, leaving only a thin outer ring of Sun visible.
Page 81: At the Barcelona Olympic Games in 1992, Derartu Tulu of Ethiopia waves a giant national flag after winning the women's ten thousand meters event.

A free interpretation of the quatrain at the beginning of this section might tell us more:

> *Woman has been hidden behind deep shadows; her brother, man, has moved through the world with hardness and heaviness, eclipsing her for so long. But this hot, iron-like property of man will cool in the feminine spirit that grows around him.*

What is becoming rapidly more evident in the last years of the twentieth century are the changes that occur when men are transformed by an overwhelming presence of feminine energy. Humanity has spent many thousands of years at war, striving to improve its material welfare and battling it out between nations and beliefs. As a result, man has damaged his world almost to the point of rendering it beyond repair. If we believe what Nostradamus tells us, then the time has now come for a very different kind of energy to patch up and transform the strife-torn world.

In the last years before the end of the millennium there might still be those who insist that the presence of a "stronger woman," in the form of the feminist movement, merely changes the players in an unchanging drama—the same roles are assumed by different players who happen to be female in character but are still essentially operating in the traditional male way. This idea is based on the fact

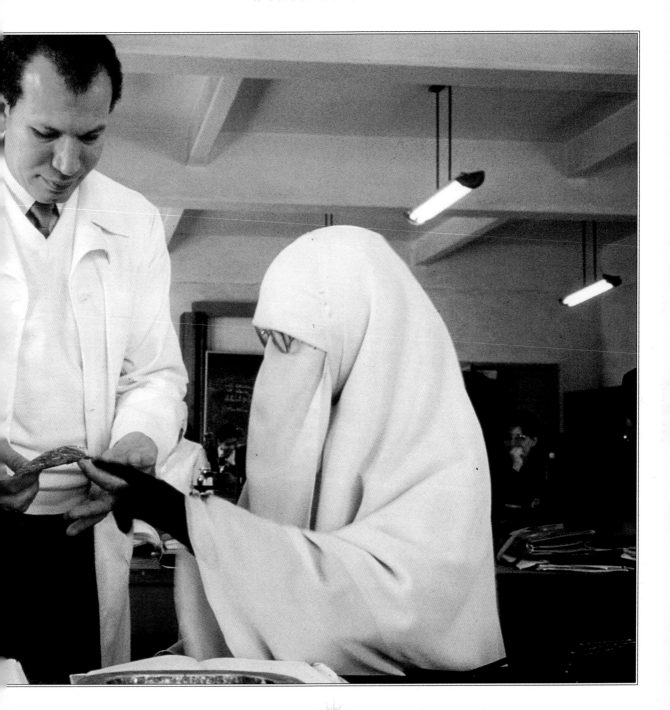

that women who presently occupy "masculine" positions, such as those in politics or religion, seem to behave like men!

In effect, the fact that there are still so few women in what can easily be observed to be "male" jobs, somehow preserves the stereotypes rather than transforms them. We might call their presence "tokenism," and tokenism certainly reduces any revolutionary drive for transformation, for it is simply drowned out by the overwhelmingly stronger male energy that exists around it.

In the United States, for example, the tiny numbers of women who are judges, chief executive officers of large corporations, doctors or politicians, have all been trained by men in organizations and schools designed and completely influenced by men and their male energy. These women must, in some part at least, have been shaped or influenced by this male-dominated pressure.

This page and opposite: The increasing number of women entering hitherto exclusively male working domains has made nonsense of the myth of male physical superiority and skill.

Right: Equal opportunities in science and engineering.
Below: Solidarity.

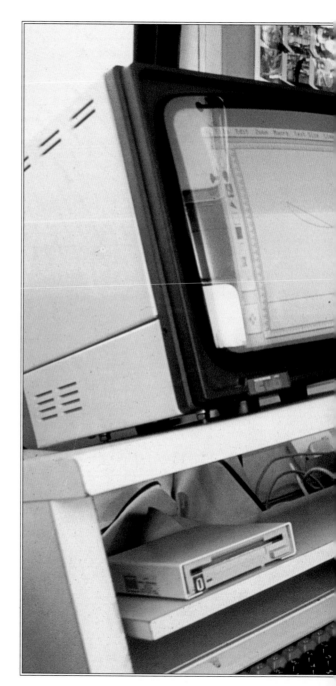

What Nostradamus is telling us in this verse, it is suggested, is that masculine energy will literally be dulled by the overwhelming presence of women in positions of influence and power, but only once a female consciousness has developed. Only at the point when this occurs will there be a major transformation of energy in the world, and a resulting change.

It is certainly quite wrong to assume that the feminist movement will somehow only create a race of women willing to accept the existing beliefs, structures and patterns of male society. The transformation caused by the presence of women will strike at the very roots of the male society that has been the norm up to the present time. The transformation that we are about to witness, in the lifetimes of most of us, is a complete rejection of patriarchal values, which will result in the total replacement of those values with something completely different.

FEMININE SHOCKWAVES

The female change will be very difficult:
City and province will gain by the change:
The heart will count most, prudence well established, chasing out cunning,
Sea, land, people will change their whole state.

CENTURY 4:21

Those who study earthquakes know that they are not sudden, unpredictable events, but the result of aeons of silent tectonic pressure. . . For a decade and a half, American women's anger had been driven underground, to smolder under the weight of the Reagan-Bush years of reaction. But while that weight kept the lid on their anger, women's psychology was changing rapidly, even as masculine power was beginning to erode.

Naomi Wolf, Fire with Fire

THE NEW PARADIGM OF A GREATER FEMALE BALANCE within the world will need very careful management, and a difficult transition will occur over the years from 1997 to 2004 when the presence of women in important positions both in world affairs and within the home will be the determining factor in the change. We may imagine that the world can handle a growing feminine energy, but most civilized countries have been dominated by men for several thousand years and various fundamental structures will alter when they cease to be in command. This change will occur most violently in countries that are still dominated by patriarchal attitudes such as those inherent in parts of the Middle East where religion totally opposes the feminine spirit.

Right and below: Although Hillary Clinton experienced difficulties in her position as a woman in power, she nevertheless helped the feminist movement to take flight in the latter years of this century.

Opposite: Sculpture in Oslo, by Gustav Vigeland.

A basic human "habit" will be dismantled during this era of change, so that underlying emotional, practical and political changes will form part of a massive experience of human renewal. This basic, underlying shift will give rise to transformations and changes in aspects of life such as science and technology, invention and innovation, creativity in the arts, birth, child-care methods and education, medicine, and the role of the aged as elders of local communities.

A free interpretation of the verse at the top of this section might be:

The change caused by the powerful presence of the female will be very difficult: but the whole world will gain by the change. The heart will be the most important feature of this transformation, but also prudence will be as much an established aspect of this new life, chasing out the cunning created by man. The entire world, in all aspects, will be altered in the most fundamental way.

Right: Oprah Winfrey—probably one of the most powerful and certainly one of the richest women in the women's movement.

The earliest visible cracks that are being seen in the massive and ancient edifice of patriarchy have occurred already in the early 1990s with judicial confrontations such as the Mike Tyson and William Kennedy Smith rape trials, and particularly the Anita Hill hearings in 1991, in which members of the United States Senate were seriously unhinged by allegations of sexual harassment.

The main feature of these cases was the evident lack of understanding, and even wild anger, amongst white males in authority at the suggestion that women might have a completely different view of reality from that of the patriarchal establishment. The pitiful lack of female representation in government in the United States and throughout most of the rest of the civilized world has now become an issue to the female population as a result of such confrontations, for they not only highlight women's lack of real power in the world, but they also reveal the true nature of male authority.

What has developed from this often necessarily aggressive stance of women in America is literally a "genderquake"–which Nostradamus' predictions echo through into the twenty-first century. This can most readily be seen in the progress made by President Clinton's pre-election campaign and the power given it by the presence of Hillary Clinton. She stands not only as a powerful female personality backing the male power position, but as an empowered individual, a lawyer in her own right, opposed to the relatively non-feminist position that had by contrast been taken by Barbara Bush while President Bush was in power. Political commentators of the time implied that the elections which put

Clinton into the White House with the Democratic party behind him were won because of the lack of understanding within the Republican party of the political importance of the female genderquake.

A formative influence in this new move towards greater feminine consciousness was the media, spear-headed by the Oprah Winfrey show, which constantly undermines patriarchal values by bringing destruc-tive male influences in the family to the forefront of American TV viewing. Women have become aware that they can actually speak about their needs and attitudes, and tell the stories of their degradation and

disadvantage to a massive and listening public, including women who still choose to remain within the conventional role of "housewife."

The most interesting aspect of Nostradamus' verses lies in his frequent references to the presence of the heart in the affairs of women in the future. Probably the single most powerful force that the feminine influence will bring, according to this interpretation of the Prophet's works, is that ultimately women will discard "cunning" and the old, very often dishonest, political methods that patriarchy has given rise to, in favor of honest, truthful and loving ways of relating in the world.

And the change is not only taking place in the United States but throughout many other parts of the world.

In the United Kingdom, the Conservative government under the leadership of John Major has been forced into providing greater opportunities for women in senior public positions by considering such devices as a Citizens' Charter for women; and there was even a suggestion by one of the earlier

Labor party leaders that there should be a Ministry
for Women, something which in the future will no
doubt be considered a normal requirement of
government everywhere.

   The reason for all this, of course, is not a sudden
shift in the attitude of the politicians occurring
because of an intrinsic change of *gestalt*, but simply
because they have been forced into an awareness of
the number of female votes "out there" which might
unseat them if they don't comply. And it will be in
this way that the political, and incidentally

probably the religious, attitudes will develop
towards what Nostradamus indicates in his predictions for the near future.

   In Australia, women's issues are being taken
increasingly seriously. Within the Australian
workforce, according to figures quoted in Naomi
Wolf's book *Fire with Fire*, women account for 41 per
cent. In addition she relates that 33 per cent of small
businesses in that country are owned by women. As a
result of acknowledging the needs that arise from
such evident dramatic growth in the influence of

Left: The Norwegian Justice Minister, Grete Faremo. In Norway, the powers of Government and Justice are both in the hands of women. How will it be when the United States undertakes this same step?

Opposite: The Prince and Princess of Wales may have undergone some major traumas during the late 1990s, but Diana provided an important role model for women in her determination to seek her own personal freedom from the restrictions of English monarchy.

women in Australian society, Paul Keating won the election in 1993.

Norway enjoys a woman Prime Minister, with seven out of the seventeen ministers being women, and half of the total police force too—a staggering change in the overall condition of the country's political and power regime resulting. The same sort of picture can be seen developing in Turkey, Spain, Sweden, and Uganda, where women's issues have created a feminine awareness in the political arena through the determined emergence of female voters.

With the rapid growth of global awareness, and the reduction in political suppression that has occurred since the end of communism in the Baltic countries, activities and changes in countries like the United States have become visible to a vast audience through television. The whole world will become increasingly aware of transformation in America and Europe in the future, so that as the world's leading and most advanced countries "get it together" to have women represented effectively, and as patriarchal values become more obviously ineffective, so the global trend will move in the same direction. In this way the feminine earthquake will grow in strength as we see out the last millennium of male domination.

CHANGES IN EDUCATION

N *MEGATRENDS FOR WOMEN*, Patricia Aburdene and John Naisbitt indicate that one of the other most important areas of change—which falls within the arena of "difficulty" which Nostradamus sees as necessary and fundamental to the growth of female awareness—will be in basic education systems, which will lead to the new paradigm of feminine equality and co-operation. Within the traditional education of the average boy at school, there has been an emphasis on the patriarchal values of achievement, independence, competitiveness and self-sufficiency; whereas for the young girl, the emphasis has always been on dependence (or co-dependence), co-operation, group orientation and home economics.

These forms of conditioning naturally tend to produce results that fit in with the social requirements of "man as bread-winner" and "woman as home-maker and child-bearer." And it is these fundamental indoctrinations that Nostradamus indicates will change. Expectations will be similar for both sexes, but there will also be a much greater emphasis on individual education, fashioned in each case for special needs.

Left: Learning young.

Below: Teaching adult literacy skills.

Opposite: Cybele, ancient mother goddess of Phrygia in Asia Minor.

3

SHE-GOD

Beneath the earth of the holy Lady the faint voice heard,
Human flame seen to shine as divine:
It will cause the earth to be stained with the blood of the lone ones [monks],
And to destroy the holy temples for the impure ones.

CENTURY 4:24

N RECENT YEARS many more divine visions of the Virgin Mary have been recorded throughout the world. Within the Catholic Church, and indeed from the Vatican itself, there is already some excitement about the idea that these increasingly frequent "visitations" signify a kind of "Second Coming" in the form of spirit guidance within the Catholic tradition. It is interesting to note that the visions are always significantly feminine. One of the most famous examples is the visions of the children in Medjugorje, in the former Yugoslavia, where the Virgin Mary appeared to the children every evening for several years. It is perhaps significant that she appeared just before the beginning of the war which split Yugoslavia into religious factions.

There are literally hundreds of other examples around the world, and we may take these either to be the Catholic "Mother of God" specifically, or perhaps, in a broader sense, the returning presence of the ancient Mother Goddess who was said to watch over

humanity in pre-Christian times.

In any event, given the human tendency to make manifest its most important myths and symbols, we may understand the increase in such apparitions to be related to the human need for a holy female presence.

Nostradamus indicates to us that during the coming decades woman's increasing importance within the established Churches and other sects does not simply signify a few women priests, but a radical change in the world view of religion and of the need for feminine remedies. In order for this to come about, women are going to overturn thousands of years of the most sexist tradition of them all—challenging the authority of the male Churches, reinterpreting the Bible, gaining ordination as a matter of course and generally integrating feminine concepts into general religious understanding.

This includes some very fundamental attitudes, and certainly a radical new look at the male-dominated Fundamentalist movement in the United States.

We may now expect a new religious understanding to occur in our near future related to personal godliness, involving literally a "She-God," which redefines the meaning of love and holiness.

Interpreted freely, the quatrain at the beginning of this chapter might read as follows:

Within the most fundamental aspects of the world which is affected by the presence of religion, a holy feminine presence will be heard as a gentle but important voice. This very human flame will be seen to shine in a divine light. Its presence will cause the world and all who live in it to be changed in a fundamental way which will include the death of the dominance of male religious influence,

This presence will destroy the established Churches of the male dominated religious forces.

This very subtle piece of prophetic writing begins with a reference to the visions of a Mother Goddess. And perhaps we may use this opportunity to go back, far back, into history, to a time long before patriarchal values were even considered. It may sound unlikely to modern man and woman, so entrenched in patriarchy as we are, that there actually was a time when attitudes engendered by competitiveness, domination and prejudice did not exist at all.

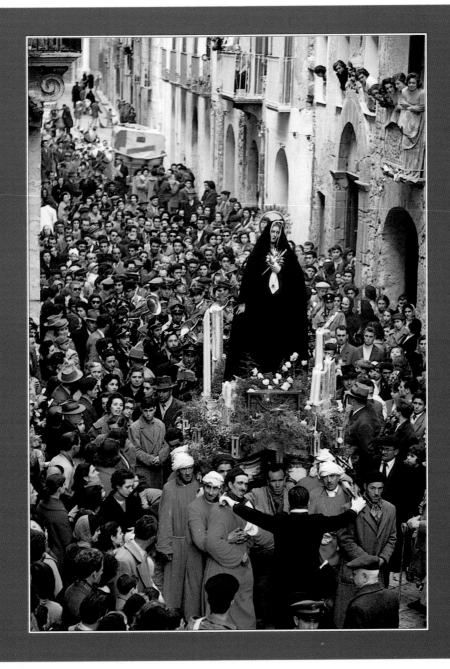

THE ANCIENT ESSENCE

ONE OF THE CHARACTERISTICS of any individual personality is that she or he will view the world through the eyes of that personality. If you are an angry person you will see the world as angry. If you are loving and simple, you will see the world as loving and simple. We are, in a sense, walking projectionists, beaming our inner aspects onto the screen of the world.

So also, we do this as whole civilizations. We are a competitive, male-oriented, dominating, aggressive society, and we tend to see the past through those eyes—often quite wrongly. Thus tombs opened in Egypt, containing elaborate burial chambers, were assumed to be those of kings, whereas in the event they turned out to be the tombs of the mothers of kings, the king himself being given lesser place.

According to quite recent discoveries, there have been successful societies in our distant past that were not patriarchal, aggressive and competitive. One such is the civilization of Minoan Crete, discovered by Sir Arthur Evans in the opening decades of this century.

Excavations on Crete between 1930 and 1980 have yielded greater detail about this socially complex and technologically advanced ancient society. In her book *The Chalice and the Blade,* Riane Eisler describes evidence of huge multi-storied palaces, homes and farms, well-organized cities and road networks. Four forms of language and writing were found—Hieroglyphic, Proto-linear, Linear A, and Linear B, which in archeological terms places Minoan society in a much more recent, historic (as opposed to pre-historic) stage of development than its period would suggest. It is

Right: Rangda, Hindu demon goddess, from Bali.
Opposite: The "Snake Goddess." Faience figurine from the Sanctuary at the Palace of Knossos, Crete.

evident that this was no ordinary, traditional civilization.

The archeologist Nicolas Platon, who had excavated in Crete for almost fifty years by 1980, uncovered a civilization that had begun before 6000 B.C. A small group of people from southwest Asia Minor had settled on the island, bringing with them the traditions of the Goddess cult, a view of life that prevailed throughout the Neolithic period. Their social and technological skills continued to develop for four thousand years, until around 2000 B.C., when Crete entered the Middle Minoan period—well into the Bronze Age, a time when the partnership concept of society, worshipping the Goddess cult, was being replaced by warlike, essentially male gods. In all the discoveries made on Crete there are no signs of war, even up to the fifteenth century B.C., when the Minoan culture was destroyed.

The essential feature of the worship of the Goddess was what Joseph Campbell called "syncretism." Put in other words, her worship was both monotheistic and polytheistic. Modern monotheistic religions such as Christianity, Islam, and Buddhism limit themselves to a God who is both male and exclusive. The Cretan and Neolithic religion was based upon a Mother Goddess who took many different forms in different civilizations but who put people in touch with nature, and was the focus of a widespread human understanding of nature as one entity.

This extraordinary unity between humanity and its environment probably originally arose out of the prehistoric need to "live off the land." The nourishing Earth was the source of birth, life and death to those who depended upon it. Prehistoric people depended first on the annual migrations of

Throughout history, but particularly in the ancient world, woman has been accorded the greatest honor in the pantheon.

Right: Image of the Neolithic Mother Goddess with the symbol of reception and overflow—the horn. From the Musée D'Aquitaine, Bordeaux, France.

Opposite: Gods of ancient Egypt— Queen Isis on the right, her lover and brother Osiris, Lord of the Underworld, and their hawk-headed son Horus. Isis was venerated as the corn and fertility goddess and worshipped as the Great Mother.

the animals, and then more directly on the cycles of the land, the seasons, the harvest, and quite naturally regarded the Earth as the source or mother of all existence.

The source was seen as essentially female in character. Thus the feminine spirit was born and became ruler of all she surveyed.

When modern feminists speak of God as a woman, this is perhaps their source, and indeed it is a much more realistic focus than any male symbol. The male God was born only out of a warlike, aggressive and competitive ethos which destroyed the Mother Goddess and literally took over the world in the Iron Age, causing the rise of large and mutually hostile empires based on conquest. This set the pattern of war and conflict between nations for the next three thousand years. Thus modern civilizations can be said to have provided largely misery and little else, other than perhaps the growth of the industrialized world, which in the light of the harmony enjoyed by ancient civilizations such as that of Crete might seem to have been a mistake.

In any event, the central religious image of the Neolithic world, which was later echoed in Crete, was that of woman giving birth rather than man dying on a cross. We could say that this is the contrast between the love of life and the fear of death. We could also hope that we might abandon the one and return to the other, and Nostradamus' verses give us the direct impression that the rebirth of the feminine spirit is the single biggest step towards that return to joy. But it is not, so far as can be interpreted from the prophet's works, a matter of changing from patriarchy to matriarchy—this would be only a switch of players while the game stays the same. The reasoning that comes to the conclusion that if patriarchal values are not present then matriarchal values must replace them is based on the assumption of domination. But domination is a male concept and will not necessarily exist in the post-patriarchal society we can envisage with the help of Nostradamus' verses.

Evidence presented in various studies, for example those undertaken by James Mellaart of the British Institute of Archeology at Ankara into pre-patriarchal Neolithic societies, shows more advanced and stable cultures worshipping within the Goddess' religious structures. These structures bore no resemblance to the dominant patriarchal cultures of the last millennia and yet were entirely peaceful, highly advanced, intelligent, and complex in nature. They represent for us a real alternative to our own social environment.

And yet it isn't as though we have not had a hint of similar social structures in our recent history. The cult of the Goddess has existed in many historical cultures. She has taken the form of the goddesses Isis and Nut in Egypt, Demeter, Kore and Hera in Greece, and more recently, as we have seen earlier, of the many apparitions of the Virgin Mary, which must surely represent a profound response to a deep and continuing awareness of the Mother Goddess.

Our awareness of these aspects of our heritage is not lacking, but the willingness to place them in

Right: God making Eve out of Adam's rib.

Opposite: The Three Marys, by Michael Wolgemut, 1499. Here we see Mary as a triple goddess in her three aspects of Maiden, Nymph and Crone.

positions of importance, high on our list of priorities, is.

We have been conditioned, and are still being conditioned by religious dogma, to believe that the power and authority of the male is more important than the female. Religion tells us that children are put on Earth by God, a male figure, and that the purpose of this is to provide fathers with, preferably, sons. Children's surnames are derived from their fathers, the inheritance of land and goods traditionally passes from father to son. Succession to the English throne passes from the monarch first to the son. We are indoctrinated by such ideas on a daily basis, because at some time in history a tremendous force was put upon the human mind to get rid of any idea that raised women above the status of chattel. Past societies, and we suggest, future societies, were and could be again, very different.

In the Minoan civilization of ancient Crete, and those earlier societies that gave rise to it in Neolithic times, for a women to be owned by a man, or even to take his name in marriage, would have seemed utterly strange.

As Nostradamus' verses gradually unfold their meaning, we begin to see that perhaps our future may be made up of a new understanding of what we have hitherto taken for granted, to our disadvantage.

Until recently we still chose to accept the misery of the man on the cross, rather than the joy of birth. But all that, according to Nostradamus, is about to change.

WOMEN AND GOD

THERE IS LITTLE DOUBT THAT WOMEN in the twentieth century are directly challenging the most sexist organizations in history—the institutions of religion.

Thousands of years of tradition, based on patriarchal values, have sustained the major religious institutions as exclusively male domains. In comparison with long past cultures such as the Neolithic, the Celtic, and others, this is a unique and very odd attitude to religion. What possible, real reasons could there be to exclude women, for example, from the priesthood? On the face of it, setting aside the traditional concepts, this exclusion seems to be an

absurdity. And according to much that we can find in Nostradamus' verses, it will come rather smartly to an end in the twenty-first century.

Oh vast Rome, your ruin approaches,
Not your walls, but your lifeblood and substance:
Someone with a sharp tongue will make a dent in you,
Harsh chains will be around it all.
CENTURY 10: 65

There are numerous verses such as this, that can be interpreted to indicate the fall of the Church of Rome. It seems more likely, however, that the

Right: A newly ordained woman priest in the Church of England.

Opposite: Joan of Arc, the young visionary from Orleans who defied Church and State to lead the French army to victory and was burnt at the stake for heresy in 1431. In this contemporary miniature she is being welcomed by Charles VII.

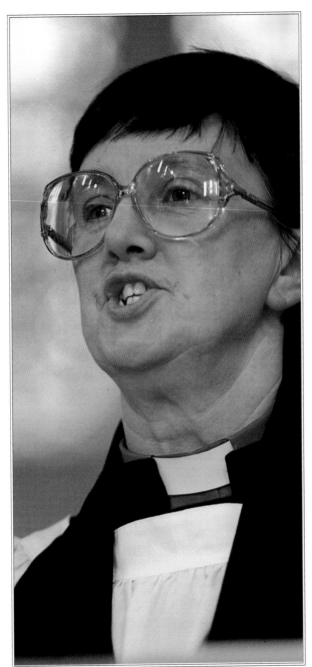

Catholic Church will not collapse completely, but will be transformed in some way; that the "lifeblood and substance" of this massive and outdated institution will find it necessary to change its structure to accommodate a changing world.

We can see something of the likely impression that women will make if we examine some of the changes that are currently taking place in the Church institutions of the world. For it won't simply be the Catholic Church that will face the demands of women, but all organized religious institutions, with a concomitant domino effect.

In November 1992, the General Synod of the Church of England voted to accept women into the priesthood. This was probably one of the

Below: Mediterranean Earth Mother figurine.

Opposite: A woman deacon spreads the gospel as women win the fight to become vicars in Britain.

biggest victories enjoyed by women in centuries, and had a major impact on the way women will be viewed in the future.

In American seminaries more than 34 per cent of students are now women, and at Yale University School of Divinity half the students are women. At Harvard University's equivalent more than 60 per cent of the students are women. These are incredible statistics, considering just how few women were involved in any aspect of organized religion just two decades ago—in fact, almost none.

According to Patricia Aburdene and John Naisbitt in *Megatrends for Women* there are now thousands of Catholic women worshipping in all-female groups today. *Non-orthodox Jewish women are embracing the traditional Orthodox mikva bath as a spiritual and women's rights ritual.*

And perhaps most dramatic of all, the American Episcopal Church elected its first woman bishop during the early 1990s.

Aburdene reports that even the American Fundamentalist movement, probably the most intransigent religious movement outside the Catholic Church, is showing signs of change, as one of the most famous TV evangelists—Pat Roberston—starts to work together with a woman—Sheila Walsh.

Within Judaism, the Reform Synagogue has already proven to be the most flexible, with women now working as rabbis and cantors, and it will perhaps not be too long before the credo of the Orthodox is altered to accommodate new female attitudes and needs.

Perhaps this is the single most relevant aspect of what the feminine spirit will do for religion—that the ancient questions will be asked again. Why should we see God as either male or female? Was it really Jesus' intention that the Christian Church should develop into a male-dominated system? Where are women in the Bible? And why has Mary, the Mother of Christ, been represented as a symbol of passivity to fit in with the patriarchal view of women?

Questions such as these are being asked by women, and form the basis of attitudes that will certainly transform the various Churches. The walls of Rome will perhaps not fall, but certainly the women's movement will alter the "lifeblood and substance" of Catholicism during the coming years.

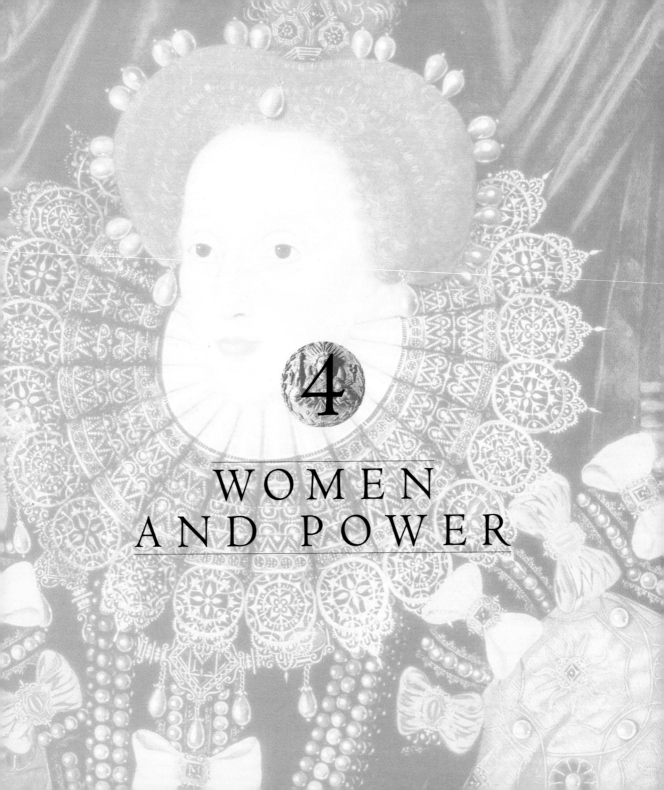

4

WOMEN
AND POWER

When Venus will be covered by the Sun
Beneath the splendor will be a hidden form:
Mercury will have exposed them to the fire,
Through warlike noise it will be insulted.

The Sun hidden eclipsed by Mercury,
Will be placed only second in the sky:
Of Vulcan Hermes she will make new pastures,
The Sun will then be seen pure, glowing and golden.

CENTURY 4:28-29

REPLICATING THE MERCURIAL SPIRIT

HE DECIPHERING OF NOSTRADAMUS' VERSES requires an understanding of the different metaphors employed. The Sun, in this and other verses, has been interpreted literally, as a metaphor for the New World, and can also imply the dominant paradigm in power at any given moment, in this case men. In this verse we find the use of the Sun and Mercury both to describe the juxtaposition of man and woman and as an alchemical metaphor. The Sun, as man, has been in the ascendancy for many centuries, but now the complex and mercurial duality of man and woman together becomes the fashion for the future. In Roman mythology Mercury (in Greek, Hermes) is the messenger of the gods, symbol of communication, and of duality—the double messages of rationality and irrationality. One of the biggest difficulties that men have faced in the past, and a reason perhaps why there is still often poor understanding between the sexes, is the apparent lack of "reason"

Right: Encounter at Safwan, southern Iraq. The uniform effectively hides the fact that this Marine is a woman.

Previous page: Mercury, messenger of the gods in ancient Greece, and the planet associated with quicksilver or an amalgam of gold and silver in alchemy.

Page 114: Elizabeth I, Queen of England. The "Armada" portrait painted by Marcus Gheeraerts the Younger, 1588.

behind feminine thought. Traditionally men have not been able to connect with feminine magic and the cyclic, often emotional changes that women undergo, and have therefore chosen to suppress these human qualities in an attempt to remain ordered and consistent. But in these short lines Nostradamus can be interpreted as telling us that the mercurial elements of life will come into closer conjunction with the Sun, man, and take a stronger position in the affairs of everyday life.

We can also interpret the same lines through an alchemical metaphor, seeing the Sun as symbolizing gold, or King (matter which must die and be reborn). In this context, Nostradamus, who was well versed in alchemy, may be telling us that king/man must die and be reborn in harmony with the feminine spirit.

Essentially this verse prophesies that men will be eclipsed by women in the near future, and that even in matters of war, policing and conflict, women will play a leading part. This is not to say, however, that the advent of feminine power will result in a continuation of the warfare that we have seen right through the twentieth century. There could be a very different scenario ahead of us.

During these days when women are still often forced to behave like men, we have seen a growth in the presence of women at war. There were 34-35,000 American women in active combat during the Gulf

War. During 1990 there were 227,018 women on active duty in the United States armed forces. If we read the verse at the beginning of this chapter carefully, it appears that this increase in the number of women in the armed forces will somehow lead to a reduction in the instance of war. It will not be that armies will slowly become less male and more female, but that, perhaps, the presence of women in the arena of conflict will cause them to help us realize that war is a purposeless activity. Perhaps we can look at a free interpretation of this verse to find hints for the future.

At a time in the future when the love of woman will be overshadowed by men, beneath the bright shining light will be a hidden form. The mercurial nature of women will already have begun to expose men to a fiery new aspect of life, and through militancy on the part of women this maleness will be exposed and insulted. Man will eventually become hidden in his turn by woman, and will be placed only second in importance. Using her newfound power she will make new pastures, and men will find a new respect in life that will make them shine again in a better light.

When Nostradamus writes about men shading a hidden form in women, we can read into this, perhaps, more than the obvious.

Let us take a look at a theory currently being examined by science.

The scientists Francisco Varela and Humberto Maturana in South America have studied what they

Right: Osho Rajneesh, one of the most influential Indian gurus of the twentieth century.

Opposite: The "maturation" phase of the alchemical process, which took a year to complete. From the Ridley manuscript.

call the "autopoesis" of living systems. Their work may be seen to be based on a hypothesis which has long been examined and understood from a less scientific viewpoint in Eastern religions such as Hinduism and some of the modern religious teachings of, for example, J. Krishnamurti and Osho Rajneesh. This is that the mind operates rather like an elaborate tape-recording machine, absorbing information and recording the results, and then acts upon those results on a perpetual, habitual level thereafter. According to this view, rather than being the masterly and vital entity upon which the Western world has based most of its understanding, the mind is little more, at least in this context, than a parrot, capable only of reiteration and lacking any originality.

Systems that are learned or imprinted upon the mind—systems such as those engendered by patriarchal society—are maintained in the human mind through a process which could be called replication. This replication, or a self-copying ability, occurs within the actual DNA code, affecting the individual at all levels of conscious and unconscious awareness—in the very cells of the body, within the psychology of individuals and thereby into the social environment which they occupy. This replication of ideas, which may not always result in the best for the individual or society, is the very basis for the maintenance of any social structure, good or bad. In a sense, we are all rather like parrots in a jungle that has been constructed by us, for our benefit or disadvantage, without true wisdom.

Right and opposite: Conformity reinforced. The replication of patriarchal culture in the West.

The biologist Rupert Sheldrake has developed a scientific (though in the current climate still regarded as renegade) theory of what he terms "morphic resonance," which describes this concept of replication in a similar way. He maintains that we are surrounded by, and contained within, habit fields which keep all the habitual functions of nature and life going simply because they have always done so. He says that a new habit—such as, for example, when the first aspirin crystals were formed—is more difficult to formulate because there is no existing morphic field to give it shape. But once the formulation is made, and repeated, so it becomes easier and easier. We can see our patriarchal morphic fields in this light. Patriarchy has been learned over a long period of time, and therefore everything within this morphic resonance is continuously repeating itself, no matter whether it is right for the occupants of the field or not.

The replicated information that leads to a patri-archal culture would not work for a culture based on partnership, for example. Patriarchal replicative thought patterns are founded on domination, aggression and fear, while the thoughts replicated for the creation of a partnership culture are based on equality, receptiveness, mutual concern and love. What two formats could be further apart than

Right: Women kick back. Graffiti on billboard.

Legs as soft and
as the day you we

these? And yet, what can be perceived from reading Nostradamus' verses is that we may be in transit from one to the other right at this moment.

The hidden form referred to in the verse is, according to this interpretation, the replicative code needed to alter society from a dominant, patriarchal mode to a partnership mode, and women are the holders of the key.

But how, we may ask, could such a change occur? Given that every single human mind would have to change in order for the new replication to have any effect, how and from what source can this transformation come about?

The simple answer lies in the fact that it has already happened before. In order for the present situation to come about, a massive new replication took place in our history, a re-replication that resulted in the transformation from a partnership culture to the present patriarchal model.

It happened, if you like, in reverse. Now we hope to reverse it again, and return to a world where the values can improve.

During the evolution of monotheism by the early Hebrews, the Christians and then the Muslims, there was massive destruction of the old partnerships created by thousands of years of pagan values. Ancient temples were destroyed, sacred Celtic tree

Below and opposite: The New World holds out hope for all.

WOMEN OF THE

groves cut down, people slaughtered, wars fought, witches burned and thousands of individuals persecuted, all in the name of a new replication of ideas that civilization believed to be the best. "Convert or die" was the theme of the Church, as we have already seen in this book.

And this has had an incredibly powerful and long-lasting effect on the individual persona—on the mind, habits, beliefs and fears of each of us. We still cross ourselves against evil, without asking why a cross, and what is evil anyway? We still, somewhere, believe in a devil and a god as the opposites which make life work. We seldom stop to ask what the source of these two entities might be, or whether they are connected. The questions have been asked:

Who made the world?

Why, God, of course.

And who created sin?

Why, the devil, of course.

And who made the devil?

Why, God, of course.

So who then is the ultimate sinner?

These connections were lost somewhere down the ages, recorded as they were in *grimoires*—books of spells—suppressed by the "word of God," now repeated by us, often parrot fashion.

So, what we may read into the lines of Nostradamus' verses is that woman rises out of the shadow and begins to help us create a new replicative code—a long, perhaps arduous, process but one that will contribute to the single biggest cultural evolutionary change to occur for over two thousand years.

Interestingly enough, a fundamental reason for the writing of this book was the realization that ancient conditioning had caused most interpreters of Nostradamus' verses to base their predictions largely on factors—such as war, conflict, fear and disaster—that are entirely familiar to a patriarchal society. Whereas if one dons the cap of an alternative, and still entirely possible, cultural system, many of the verses read totally differently. We see largely through the eyes of our beliefs, and only with some determination can we begin to discern shadows which may be hidden by the overwhelming light of pre-existing conditioning—the current dominant replication.

We read on in this verse that:

The mercurial nature of women will already have begun to expose men to a fiery new aspect of life, and through militancy on the part of women this maleness will be exposed and insulted.

This echo of the earlier verses relating to the march of the Seline Movement across Europe—the militancy on the part of women—helps to portray the more mercurial aspect of the feminine spirit, a characteristic that many of us, both male and female, will welcome, but many may not!

Man will eventually become hidden in his turn by woman, and will be placed only second in importance. Using her newfound power she will make new pastures, and men will find a new respect in life that will make them shine again in a better light.

But everything that goes around, comes around again, and men, though hidden in their turn by the much increased strength of the female spirit, will come back into their own in a more equal and balanced manner, and thereby find greater respect for life. Perhaps this will be the decisive change, which will contribute in turn to an improvement in the present levels of global pollution—the result of a respect for birth and life rather than suffering and death. In order for this to happen, it is likely that the groundswell of new female voters will influence the political power positions of the world—most likely in the form of a female American president.

127

THE FIRST FEMALE PRESIDENT OF THE UNITED STATES

The Moon in the full of night over the high mountain,
The new wise one with a lone brain seen there:
By her disciples invited to be immortal,
Eyes at noon. Hands on bosoms, bodies in the fire.

CENTURY 4: 31

THIS SLIGHTLY OBSCURE VERSE begins our hunt for a female president of the United States. Perhaps the most important single clue in the verse lies in the original French version which employs the word *sophe* in the second line—*Le nouveau sophe d'un seul cerveau la vu.* The word derives from both Greek and Latin—*sophos*—and means "wise one." On a simple level Nostradamus could plainly have been indicating the presence of a wise individual with a good brain *(cerveau)*, which stands alone *(seul).*

She is, according to the third line, invited by her disciples, or supporters, to become immortal. She is seen (or is watching) either at noon or to the south, her hands on her bosom and her body in the fire. What can all this mean?

The first words in this line in the French version read *Yeux au midi.* This can either mean: "eyes at midday," or it could also mean "eyes to the south." If we accept the version that tells us "eyes to the south," we might suppose that this individual, a woman,

who will be made immortal by her followers, will come from the south of the United States.

On the day that all this comes to fruition, the moon is full and seen over a high mountain.

There is only one more United States election in this millennium—in 1996. If President Clinton is re-elected for his second term then, the next date for a likely political change is the millennial year 2000, when elections fall again. This time, however, he will not be able, under the American constitution, to stand again. Whether Clinton or a Republican candidate becomes the next president, a lot of energy will build up against the patriarchal, male-dominated values of the past in the last four years of

the millennium, and by November 2000 it seems likely that a female candidate will have found her way to the podium.

Given these general observations and the specific hints in the quatrain, the suggestion is that Nostradamus' verse is guiding us towards a location for the first female president in the southern regions of the United States. There are, of course, from a political point of view, a number of candidates for this position, and we can only conjecture as to who might get the job. One of the possible candidates in that part of the country during the latter years of the twentieth century lives in Texas. It is suggested therefore that in November of the year 2000 one

Left: Ann Richards—one of the candidates for the first female president of the United States, according to an interpretation of Nostradamus.

Previous pages: The Statue of Liberty illuminated by fireworks marking her hundredth birthday; and the Clintons and Tipper Gore at a ceremony to thank supporters of the American Health Security Act.

possible candidate who may succeed to the American presidency, as the first ever woman to do so, is Ann Willis Richards, ex-Governor of Texas. There are a number of people within the political women's sectors of the United States who would support such a result. Patricia Aburdene and John Naisbitt, in their book, state the following under the heading *Women to Watch:*

Who can resist speculating on who will become the first woman president? Will she be a Republican or a Democrat? Will she ascend to the presidency after serving as vice president?

...Many would welcome Governor Ann Richards' wit and outstanding speaking ability on the presidential campaign trail. In that department, she is certainly superior to every presidential candidate in recent history.

It is not at all certain that President Clinton will be re-elected in 1996, so it is not at all clear how Ann Richards would reach the presidency, but she has the right political and feminist background to be the choice. Born in 1933 in Waco, Texas, she was the keynote speaker at the Democratic National Convention in 1988 and named Woman of the Year in

Texas that same year. She wrote *Straight from the Heart,* an important women's liberation book in 1989, and her record as Governor of Texas puts her in an ideal position to gain women's votes.

Additional detail may help to give shape to the prediction. Perhaps the final celebrations for the winner in the year 2000 will be held near a mountain or high hill at night at a full moon. Perhaps, in her elation at the result, she will place her hands across her bosom (in any event this is probably allegorical). For certain, the first woman to become President of the United States will be "in the fire" of political conflict from the very moment she steps into her new position. And, as we shall see in Chapter Six, there are other prophecies in Nostradamus' writings that strengthen this interpretation. The above is, of course, largely conjecture, as Nostradamus' prophetic vision is, as ever, vague and convoluted. Other possible candidates include Barbara Boxer, Governor of California, though purely from the standpoint of Nostradamus' verses, this name does not fit quite so well.

There is no certainty, of course, that this first female president will be a successful one, and in fact there are a number of verses in the Centuries which indicate that she will have many problems and perhaps end up something of a failure.

When the eclipse of the Sun will have occurred,
The monster will be seen in the fulness of the day:
In quite another way will it be interpreted,
A high price unguarded and none will have foreseen it.
CENTURY 3:34

This verse gives us the impression that once woman has managed to take a more powerful and more equal role in government (after the Sun, man, is eclipsed), once she is seen in the full light of day, she turns out, perhaps, whoever she may be in this particular case, to be a monster! And in the passion of the feminist movement, no one would have predicted that the first woman to succeed to power would end up not succeeding in power. But more of that later.

5

THE SECRET
SOCIETY
OF WOMEN

By means of the supreme power of eternal God, we are led by the Moon: before she has completed her entire cycle, the Sun will come and then Saturn. For according to the signs of the heavens, the reign of Saturn will return; so that all told, the world is drawing near to an anaragonic revolution.

PREFACE TO HIS SON CÉSAR.

The embattled gates to equal rights have indeed opened up for modern women, but I sometimes think to myself: "That is not what I meant by freedom—it is only social progress."

Sonya Rudikoff

THROUGHOUT THE RECENT HISTORY OF THE WEST there have been many secret societies. We have seen the Gnostics, the Knights Templar, the Rosicrucians, and many others, including even heretical messianic sects within Judaism, which have been forced by necessity to remain in the protection of the shadows because of persecution by other belief systems. These secret "societies" concealed themselves from the repression of moralistic attitudes which they could not support, but also could not stand up against. In order to sustain their own credos and beliefs, they often built whole social structures in secret, with rules and laws devised to govern the embattled few who were sustained by the knowledge of compatriotism and the drama and tension of secrecy. For some years in America similar structures were created by repressed minorities, such as black people and, subsequently, the gay community.

Left and previous pages: Minority groups have traditionally formed secret sub cultures in self defence against the dominant paradigm. Increasingly gay people are asserting their right to liberty and acceptance.

Page 134: Fresco of dancing women dating from the fifth century B.C., from an Etruscan tomb in Ruvo, Italy. In the National Archeological Museum, Milan.

Wherever a particular unit is under fire from the larger society, it will tend to gather in groups to find mutual support. Society as a whole is essentially like a giant, and often monstrous, animal. It will support only those that adhere to its rules. Religious cults down the ages (including Christianity) have suffered at the hands of this monster, and only by enough determination, energy and force, have minority groups surfaced to find a place in, and so alter, the society they initially disrupted.

In Chapter One we discussed the verses prophesying a movement of women which would result in a mass march across parts of Europe, and called it the Seline Movement.

The quatrains give a strong sense of a band of women who have gathered together to make the march occur. This band is not simply seeking equal rights in a male-dominated society, but complete freedom to function in all respects on equal terms with men. This is yet to come.

Nostradamus' words give a definite sense of conspiracy—*the badly conceived secret* is mentioned—and there is a feeling of common purpose, as the gathering of women determines to make an impact on the society that has suppressed them for so many centuries. In essence, events, such as the Seline March, and the election of the first American female president, are leading up to the

Below: Identifying with the Scarlet Woman—coming out with a vengeance.

Opposite: Secrets of the Heart. A painting by Brooklyn artist Daniel Koubel.

emergence of women into society, out of secrecy. In the last decades of the twentieth century women have, in effect, had to create a secret society amongst themselves and only in the latter years of this century and the early years of the next will they come out of the closet, so to speak.

This interpretation of Century 2:73-82 is reinforced by another part of Nostradamus' prophetic work—a letter to his son Caesar, a few lines of which are set out at the head of this chapter. Let us consider these step by step.

By means of the supreme power of eternal God, we are led by the Moon:

Nostradamus makes references to the Moon throughout his prophecies, and although this occasionally refers to the Moon itself, there are far more instances of the use of the Moon as a metaphor for the state of womankind. Lunar cycles are too short to be

used as an astrological directive for timing the prophecies, so we can assume that in this case, Nostradamus is referring to the Moon metaphorically. Thus, we are led by woman. This may be so in any event, but it is particularly so in relation to a future where the feminine spirit has grown in strength in the world.

...before she has completed her entire cycle, the Sun will come and then Saturn.

Nostradamus tells us that the newfound power of women will be rising, that it will not have completed its full cycle of transformation, when men (the Sun) return to a position of equality once again.

For many men during the late twentieth century, feminism has posed problems, in the sense that they have frequently felt diminished by the crimes and mistakes that their past has imposed upon them. The male of our species has been forced to re-examine his sexuality, his power, his ego and many, if not most, of his previously established attitudes. As feminism

ical description, for in astrological interpretation Saturn is generally associated with the male planets. But this has arisen only because the patriarchal attitude of the interpreters has dictated it. True, in Greek mythology the Titan Cronus (in Latin, Saturn), castrated his father Uranus and swallowed his own children (so becoming identified with Time, the devourer of all things). However, in a war with the gods led by Zeus, he was defeated and withdrew with the Titans to found a kingdom in the farthest west. Thus, the power associated with the planet Saturn was, in ancient Greece, that of peace. For Saturn has an earth energy, and earth energies are almost always feminine. Astrologically Saturn rules Capricorn, a feminine, earth sign, and Saturn is also concerned (among other things) with conservation and maintenance—again, feminine characteristics. What Nostradamus indicates here is the return of harmony after conflict.

For anyone who knows a little about modern astrology, one of the most troublesome and complex periods of any young individual's life is the point at which Saturn returns. Put another way—when we are born, Saturn is in a particular part of our astrological environment, and on its recurring course through the heavens and through our lives, this exact position occurs on the next full orbit around Earth. This takes approximately twenty-eight years. The period of the

takes a stronger hold in the worlds of politics, the Church and business, so the disenfranchisement of the male will be felt still more greatly. But eventually the pendulum will swing back and men will begin to understand that there is a place in the world for them beside women rather than above them, as they imagined themselves to be in the past. New attitudes for women will produce new attitudes for men.

Finally in this line we are told that Saturn will return also. This is a fascinating piece of metaphor-

Saturn return can often be a traumatic one for an individual, and at around twenty-eight years of age, when we reach the beginning of the fifth seven-year cycle, we very often reach a stage in our lives where dramatic, sometimes painful change occurs. This Saturn return is seen in astrology as an event which stands apart from the characteristics of the planet Saturn, and therefore we can accept perhaps that Nostradamus was giving us a series of metaphors and warnings within the one reference to the planet.

We can deduce, therefore, that Nostradamus may be telling us that the Saturn return of the feminist movement will occur once men have come back to some form of equality, after the women's movement has made its mark. At this point women will encounter problems with their newfound positions in life and in the new society they have helped to create. If we suppose that the real women's movement began in the early 1990s, we can project this prophecy as taking effect towards the end of the second decade of the next millennium. The last line in this piece then adds a strange, enigmatic finale:

For according to the signs of the heavens, the reign of Saturn will return; so that all told, the world is drawing near to an anaragonic revolution.

The word "anaragonic" has troubled interpreters of Nostradamus' prophecies from the very beginning.

Edgar Leoni, perhaps the most thorough of the recent interpreters, suggests that La Pelletier's earlier interpretation may be correct and that the word derives from the Greek words *anairesin-gonichos* which mean "destruction-engendering." This idea, given that it bears only a remote and somewhat tortuous resemblance to the pseudo-French word in Nostradamus' text probably mostly derives from the war-conscious mind of the twentieth century.

Another interpretation comes from Fortune Rigaud, who suggests that the word either grew out of the Greek word *anax-agora,* which means a sovereign mob, or *Anaxagoras,* the name of the Greek philosopher and tutor of Pericles, who predicted the end of the world through fire and water. Nostradamus, however, would not have intended such a description to be taken at face value.

As discussed in another, recent book by the author, *Nostradamus—the Millennium and Beyond,* end-of-the-world scenarios are a subject of great interest, possibly because they become a macrocosmic version of the individual human fear of death. We project our personal fears upon the world. We expect that the world will end in some shattering and apocalyptic cataclysm, probably brought about either by the pressing of a certain "red button" by a foolish politician, or as a result of the wanton neglect of our environment. We suppose that we have sufficient

Opposite: The triumph of Christian Spain. After trial by the Inquisition came public repentance and punishment. The *auto-da-fé,* or "act of the faith," was a ceremony held in the main square and attended by high and low.

power to overcome the natural power of the cosmos, and that our dream of disaster will be greater than the dream the cosmos has of itself. And this tendency, reaches a peak towards the end of a millennium.

The most likely solution can be found when we consider Nostradamus' own time. The Greek prefix *an-* means "not," or "without." Thus, *anaragonique* means "not Aragonic." What, then, was the "Aragonic" revolution?

When Ferdinand II of Aragon married Isabella of Castile in 1469, so uniting the two kingdoms, Spain became one of the greatest powers in the world. Having expelled the Moors and Jews in the name of religious and racial purity, and established the infamous Spanish Inquisition, they were granted the title of *los reyes católicos,* "the Catholic kings." Under their successors, Charles I and Philip II, the Spanish maritime empire controlled Central and South America, Naples, Sicily, Milan, and the Netherlands, and posed a permanent threat to France. Such a rapid rise in fortunes and shift of power must have seemed to Spain's neighbors nothing less than revolutionary. Conquering in the name of God, the

most aggressively patriarchal power in Europe seemed to be reaping the rewards of greed, intolerance and military might.

Nostradamus was wise enough to see beyond this. The "unaragonic revolution" he was referring to embodies the opposite attributes. It is that peaceful revolution which will occur when the feminine spirit finally triumphs over the masculine and gives humanity its first real glimpse of wisdom, a wisdom that it has profoundly lacked until now.

This revolution will certainly mean the end of the world as we know it, though this may not be apparent to all of us. But those who are watching the way the world evolves will undoubtedly notice, for this could be the single biggest revolution the world has ever known. It will arise from the Secret Society of Women, which already exists. Unlike male secret societies, however, the feminine version needs no written constitution, no fixed rules, and no central government, for the Secret Society of Women is an unspoken, mutable bond which could not be sustained by the male spirit. It has no boundaries and thereby makes no wars.

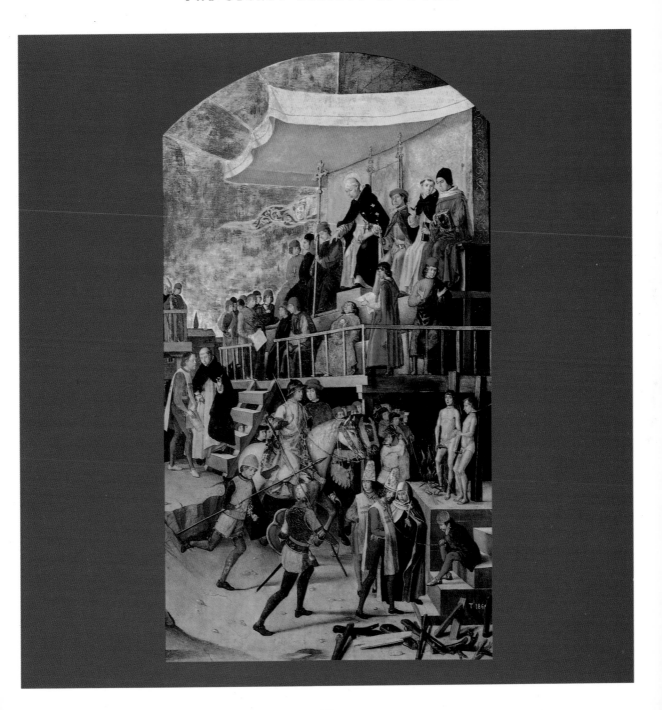

FEMININE MAGIC

A GROWING FEATURE OF THE LATTER YEARS of the twentieth century is the apparent increase in the occurrence of unexplained phenomena. There have been more reported sightings of UFOs, more ghost hunts, more bizarre, often apparently impossible happenings in recent years than in the past hundred. There are corn circles, extraordinary and precise earth-markings in Europe and the United States, which, despite the attempts of rationalists and skeptics such as James Randi, still defy real explanation. There are literally thousands of reports of UFO sightings and alien encounters, numerous ghostly apparitions, and reports of events that cannot be explained within normal scientific parameters.

What is perhaps not understood by those who seek to discount such phenomena is the revived human need to believe in magic. The scientific age and the modern passion for the deification of the mind has temporarily spoiled our belief in the irrational, the instinctual, the magical, and the inexplicable. Our fundamental, renewed interest in such things is an expression of the irrepressible human love of mystery.

The return, once again, of women to center stage will bring back that lost magic, and help create a world where logic and rationality are subsumed by beauty, taste and magic spells!

Magical capability is predominantly a female quality, though this does not mean that men do not possess it in some measure. Sadly, the overimportance of science, technology and the pressures of a competitive, aggressive world, seem to reduce the instinctual capacity in men, and so there has been a tendency in the past, and there still is in the present, though perhaps less so, for those in command to suppress these so-called "useless" qualities in women.

But Nostradamus has something to say about this too.

The lover's heart is opened by furtive love
The woman ravished by floods of tears:
The lascivious will mimic
with moral indignation,
The father will twice do without the soul.
CENTURY 8: 25

This verse is a classic amongst Nostradamus' quatrains, for it leaves almost all interpreters completely at a loss. First, it doesn't fit with the "warring" viewpoint of our twentieth-century fears. Nobody seems to be dying, and no battles are being fought. There is no end-of-the-world scenario and nothing in the midst of a catastrophic plague. And secondly, it is difficult to interpret from within a patriarchal conditioning, being about love, sex, and the soul.

These subjects may well acquire the greatest significance of all, once the feminine perspective prevails. Men have not, generally speaking, paid a great deal of attention to love or the soul as issues in the past. They have paid attention to sex, but in a way that has caused much heartache, largely through the suppression of the natural sexuality that is available within the human psyche, or put another way, the male-dominated societies have chosen to suppress female sexuality.

Patriarchal society has attempted to reduce our openness, to fetter our free sexual spirits with shameful, furtive attitudes, starting from the very earliest age.

Education has taken the form of heavily conditioned, often porno-graphic (sex without love) messages. American society as a whole displays a strange imbalance of sexual display and

Left: Metal woman, Las Vegas.

Opposite: Diana Ross performing at the inauguration of President-elect Clinton.

repression, with every newsstand and cinema offering an unlimited range of the weirdest, most revolting and "kinky" sexuality to the public, while at the same time the "normal" attitude to sex is very much "under the counter," preferring to sneer at human intimacy.

This distorted approach to sexuality and love is derived from a deeply ingrained conditioning, largely brought about by organized religious dogma, which has attached sex to sin, as though the most fundamental activity of human nature were somehow bad!

It is not that we truly believe it to be bad when we consider it soberly, but our unconscious attitudes are so deeply ingrained that we habitually react as though we think it bad.

This unconscious attitude is transmitted to our offspring equally unconsciously. It is not that we really mean to pass on such nonsense, but without realizing it parents will avoid direct explanation of sexual behavior (particularly their own, about which they are invariably

embarrassed) because they don't understand how it works themselves, so they inevitably educate their children in the light of this poor knowledge.

Sexual education within our school systems, even in the last years of the twentieth century, still carries a strong element of guilt and so creates confusion amongst pupils; and the pupils themselves often educate one another in ways that are so confused, unhappy and furtive that the result can take years to put right, and may never be completely cleared out of the adult psyche.

And what is worst of all about this cycle of behavior is the fact that sex is connected with the emotions. It is connected with love and the soul, and if the basic understanding of sexuality is besmirched by foolish education, the individual becomes unable to love effectively, unable to express emotions properly and freely, and therefore unable to grasp the inspiration which is available from the soul itself. There is, in effect, a battlement built up around the individual psyche that will neither let anything fresh and innocent in, nor allow true emanations of feelings and moods out.

What we have in the verse at the beginning of this section is a direct reference to the effects of the death of patriarchy. Let us take the lines more freely:

The heart is opened because of a furtive love, and by the fact that women have so long been ravished by floods of tears. The lascivious of the past will parody this development with moral indignation, and the patriarchal world will realize that it has so long done without the soul.

Having tired of sexual repression, our true sexuality will eventually be liberated, by the greater presence of the feminine spirit. Hypocrites who continue to pretend moral indignation because of religious attitudes or false social controls, will sneer still, because, however free a society may be, there will always be the negative and foolish element somewhere. But most important of all, in the last line, patriarchal attitudes (the father in the original verse) will yield gladly once women demonstrate the true value of natural and free sexuality, which gives access to the soul, to inspiration, and most of all to love—which, however clichéd it may sound, is the only cure.

6

TRANSFORMING
THE WORLD

Before long all will be rearranged,
We can hope for a very sinister century,
The estate that was masked and alone will change,
Few will wish to stay as they were.

CENTURY 2: 10

WE HAVE SEEN IN EARLIER CHAPTERS some of the ways in which women will move in large numbers into higher and more influential positions in society—in politics, the priesthood and business—while maintaining their essential difference from the patriarchal past.

Our society remains, at the end of the twentieth century, very much a society of men. Attitudes are still almost completely patriarchal, for patriarchy as a system has been around too long to be disposed of or transformed so quickly. The whole preoccupation with war, with armies, for example, is based on a patriarchal, protective concept, that somehow we need either to fight with or to defend against one another in order to live safely.

Nations are ruled by men's ideas, ideas of aggression, domination, fear. We have seen that such ideas are not the only models for effective rule and order. In fact, the ideas themselves are what help to perpetuate the aggression, domination, and fear. There are other ways, but we have lived in patriarchies for so long that we have forgotten the alternatives. According to Nostradamus, and other prophets, our present social structures will fall by the wayside as women bring a greater influence to the world in numbers, and in determination. A critical mass is needed for this to occur.

The process will still take time and struggle, though in this age of rapid change it will not be so long that most of us will not live to see the prophecy at the beginning of this chapter fulfilled.

Having seen something of the ways in which women will acquire greater influence, we are now able to look at the changes that will occur as a result of that influence. Nostradamus has helped us to envisage a fresh paradigm, a non-patriarchal society on Earth for the first time in thousands of years.

OPENING THE DOORS TO THE FEMININE

IRST PERHAPS WE CAN TRY TO SEE what might emerge from a critical mass of the feminine spirit. Where and how would such a transformation of energy impact on our world? What feminine characteristics would we find predominant after this change?

In order to identify potential characteristics of the emergent femininity, we will take note of some of the best feminist writing of the last few years. Once we have made a brief "list," we will seek advice from Nostradamus, by looking at relevant verses from his *Centuries.*

We are all familiar with legends about an earlier, more harmonious and peaceful age. The Bible tells of a garden where woman and man lived in harmony with each other and nature—before a male god decreed that woman henceforth be subservient to man. The Chinese Tao Te Ching *describes a time when the yin, or feminine principle, was not yet ruled by the male principle, the yang, a time when the wisdom of the mother was still honored and followed above all.*

Riane Eisler, The Chalice and the Blade

Harmony, then, may be considered a potential characteristic of this new society.

Harmony arises out of balance and acceptance, and out of learning to put aspects of human nature, such as domination, competitive anxiety, and mutual concern, in their proper places.

Left: Rally for funding breast cancer research.

Previous page: Flying the flag at the third Olympiad in California.

Page 156: Female Buddhist retreatant receiving blessing from the retreat master at Kagyu monastery in France.

This is not to say that the competitive spirit will disappear, or that individuals will not continue to be dominating or anxious, but these characteristics may be seen as existing in minority situations, not predominating in government, Church and State as they do today.

Nostradamus tells us that *few will wish to stay as they were.* While we may look forward to a new world in which the change is for the better, some may cling to the familiar life of misery that has been engendered by patriarchy. After all, we can grow attached to our neuroses.

In every dimension of life there is a sense of old molds cracked or cracking, of the precious—or rancid—contents spilling out, but there is no vision of a human future....
Humans have reached a stage from which it is almost impossible to imagine a future...we are utterly bankrupt of vision. And the barrenness of our imagination, our hope and faith, could result in the annihilation of our race.
This book rests on the assumptions that our present lack of vision as well as the present condition of the world is the result of the failure of our morality; that it is possible for humans to create and live by a different morality; and that only by adopting a new morality can we restore enough emotional, physical and intellectual equilibrium to create a more felicitous society.

Marilyn French, Beyond Power

Second, then, in our list of important characteristics of the feminine new world is a *new morality*. The first line of the quatrain at the beginning of this chapter tells us that *Before long all will be rearranged*. One of those rearrangements will have to be a new morality, and that morality perhaps will come from a completely new viewpoint, provided by the acceptance and acknowledgment of the ancient ways that grew out of respect for the Mother Goddess.

As women and men re-sort out the issues that have divided them, and seek a deeper, more creative level of partnership, men will want and need to know about the trends shaping womens lives, about the new activities women engage in.

Patricia Aburdene and
John Naisbitt,
Megatrends for Women

Right: Ancient goddess figurine.

Opposite: Mother of the Universe,
symbol of the eternal feminine,
by the sculptor Deva Shika.

Third comes *co-operation* between men and women, and a genuine desire in men to know what women are about, and what they need in life. This attitude has been singularly lacking in the past, and only very recently have men begun to give up belittling the efforts of women because of their fear of inferiority. Fear of inferiority and the compulsion to belittle arise out of a need to control, and co-operation requires no control. It either comes naturally or it doesn't exist. Most of the wars that are still being fought around the world arise out of the absurd notion that land can be owned by people, that a country should have more land under its control than it already has. This concept was given birth to the day men decided to parcel up territory for the benefit of their sons. Co-operation would ameliorate and monitor this possessive tendency in different ways, perhaps by opening up borders, as has occurred for example in Europe.

And on the more practical side:

Women lack a positive emotional vocabulary about money. While many great stories about men are stories about the romance between men and riches, women have very little narrative relationship to the idea of wealth, or the drama of seeking, building or losing a fortune.
Naomi Wolf, Fire with Fire

Nostradamus, in the verse at the top of this chapter, tells us that *The estate that was masked and alone will change,* and one of the ways that it will have to change is towards a much greater degree of involvement by women in the global economy, for essentially men have made a terrible mess of this vital aspect of human affairs. Before the genderquake reaches a stage of co-operation and harmony it will need to go through a period of *discovery*, specifically in relation to financial and political behavior. It may not

Left: Diane Feinstein, another possible candidate for the first female US president, at a campaign against domestic violence in San Francisco, 1992.

be enough for women to equal men in their knowledge of economics, for this would only mean a continuation of financial inequality around the world, a continuation of starvation, poverty for the majority, and vast, unnecessary wealth in the hands of a tiny minority.

One of the characteristics that will enhance this new feminine world will therefore be a willingness to discover and thereby *innovate.*

Adam Maxwell, age twenty-four, husband to Ruth. A boy who wants to go to the top. As if the world has a top!
Octavia Waldo, Roman Spring

Contrary to popular conceptions, probably the greatest contribution of the feminine paradigm in the future will be its *spirituality.* Women will help men to understand that their ambitions are not the be-all and end-all of life. And for men, this will begin by being a "very sinister" change, for men take their ambitions very seriously indeed. This is not to say

The new assertive woman will
be a catalyst for change.

that women don't also take ambition seriously,
because they are still strongly influenced by patriarchy. Once the critical mass is reached, many of
these things will change.

So we are looking, perhaps, for a world that will
eventually, because of the feminine spirit, reach a new
estate—one that contains harmony, in at least a
greater measure than today, and co-operation between
nations, people, races. It will also develop new ways of
looking at the fundamental aspects of industry and
economics, such as the way money is related to
human effort. And finally women will bring a new
spirituality and maturity to society, helping men to
learn the truth about ambition, domination and
competition, and so avoid replicating all the same
habits, generation after generation.

THE GREAT DAME IS BORN

 NE OF NOSTRADAMUS' MOST DRAMATIC SERIES of prophecies occurs in an "Epistle" he wrote to Henry II, the King of France, during the latter part of his life. This remarkable document literally outlines the future history of the world. In many parts it is so accurate that it leaves the reader astonished, for Nostradamus set out the future in a way that no other prophet had ever done, or has done since.

Right: Mary, Queen of Scots, niece of the powerful Guise brothers and wife of Francis II of France. By the Elizabethan miniaturist Nicholas Hilliard, c. 1578.

Opposite: "Marianne," personification of the French Republic. The Great Dame mentioned in Nostradamus' Epistle has been interpreted as being relevant to the fate of France.

Some pages into the very long letter, there are a few lines that concern our subject, and they read as follows:

For God will pay attention to the long barrenness of the great dame, who will conceive two principal children. But she will be at risk, and the female she will give birth to will also, because of the fears of the age, be at risk of death by the age of eighteen years, and will not survive beyond thirty-six years. She will leave three males, and one female, and of these two will not have had the same father.

There will be great differences between the three brothers, and then there will be great co-operation and agreement between them that three and four parts of Europe will be disrupted. The youngest one will help to sustain the Christian Church and beneath him new sects will be elevated and then will fall, Arabs will be driven away, kingdoms united and new laws made.

THE EPISTLE TO HENRY II

The debate surrounding these words, and those in the rest of the Epistle to Henry II, has continued since Nostradamus was first interpreted. Is the "Great Dame" related to France? Or is she related to communism, or fascism, or Europe, or the French Queen, Catherine de' Medici? Are the two principal children chosen from among Catherine's seven surviving offspring—could they be Francis II, perhaps, and Elizabeth, who married Philip II of Spain? Who will this child be that sustains the Christian Church, and what will the sects be that come and go beneath him?

None of these questions has ever been answered effectively . There have not been, since Nostradamus' time, any kings who fit the above description. Nor have there been any events that accord with the passage.

Of course, we could say that Nostradamus simply got it wrong, and leave it there. But so much of the rest of the Epistle has proved accurate that we may presume that if this part of it has not been borne out by events, it is simply because they have not yet occurred.

It is the authors contention that these lines apply to events, specific in nature, in our future, and that they relate to the major influence of feminism, partly forming an allegory of what we will see happen during the early years of the twenty-first century, and partly relating specifically to individuals in our future.

The prophecy begins with an allegory with a clear meaning—that the *great dame,* which we can easily interpret as woman, will *conceive two principal children.* Nostradamus does not say "give birth to" two children, and they are not just children, but principal children.

The French word *concevoir* can also mean "to design," so it is entirely possible that Nostradamus was telling us of a grand design by woman to create two new principles.

God will pay attention to the long barrenness of woman, who will design two new principles.

Next we read that this "barren woman," the allegorical feminine spirit that has so long been neglected by the world (and certainly by God), although she will have conceived these two principles, will soon be in danger—some eighteen years after the principles have been conceived.

But she will be at risk, and the female she will give birth to will also, because of the fears of the age, be at risk of death by the age of eighteen years, and will not survive beyond thirty-six years.

And these principles will not work beyond thirty-six years. If we go back to our established time-line—where we decided that the beginning of the real

feminist movement occurred in the early 1990s—then the women's movement will, by this interpretation, start to show cracks around the year 2008, and by 2026 will have failed, at least in terms of the principles that were conceived in the early years.

But it is also suggested that Nostradamus was not merely giving us an allegorical statement, but linking it to actual individuals in our future. The logic behind this is derived from the fact that we are given a kind of lineage in the lines that follow.

She will leave three males, and one female, and of these, two will not have had the same father.

We mentioned the date 2008 as being the beginning of some sort of downfall, or further transformation, of the feminist movement. This year happens to be the

end of the second term of our proposed first woman president of the United States, who we have suggested might be Ann Richards, the former Governor of Texas, or Barbara Boxer, the Governor of California. It is also worth noting that if we take Nostradamus' information literally, then the first woman president of the United States should have four children, *three males, and one female*. Ann Richards has four children, Cecile, Daniel, Clarke and Ellen—two boys and two girls—perhaps close enough! It is not suggested that two of them had different fathers, but they might each have followed a different spiritual mentor.

There will be great differences between the three brothers, and then there will be great co-operation and agreement between them that three and four parts of Europe will be disrupted. The youngest one will help to sustain the Christian Church and beneath him new sects will be elevated and then will fall, Arabs will be driven away, kingdoms united and new laws made.

There are similarities between this prophetic Epistle and the verses that we examined earlier surrounding the Seline Movement and the march across Europe.

Left: Ann Richards, ex-Governor of Texas – possible candidate for future President?

In that series we found mention of three wreaths and three sisters, which were also interpreted allegorically as relating to the banner of the Seline Movement and the principles of femininity.

In this case we read of three sons and a daughter being born out of the established women's movement or an individual within it, and further hints inform us that there will be great *co-operation* between these three sons, so that much of Europe will be affected. Could these children be the offspring of a prominent female figure in world politics? Could they in fact become famous individuals, who will work in politics in the coming years, following in the footsteps of their mother? This would already be a major step for the feminine revolution, for in the past patriarchal society has dictated the pattern "like father, like son." Perhaps now we may coin a new cliché—"like mother, like child." In any event, if we are to believe in this prophecy, and if it is more than coincidence that our first female president of the United States, if we have the correct name, has four children, then perhaps those four children will be instrumental in the affairs of Europe and of the Christian Church during the first few decades of the twenty-first century.

FEMALE LINES

FTER PROPHESYING THE PRESENCE OF A *GREAT DAME* who gives birth to four children, the Epistle to Henry II continues on the same theme. It seems, if we interpret the words correctly, that the children of the first woman president of the United States are active in a number of important national and international arenas during the first decades of the twenty-first century. It can also be shown that their positions in the political and religious worlds of the United States and Europe enable them to further the progress of feminine power in the future. We will examine each set of lines in turn.

> *The oldest child will be involved with the country whose banner shows angry crowned lions with paws resting on intrepid arms. The second child in age will run far, in accompaniment with Latin people, until a second and furious path is taken to Mount Louis. From here he will go down to then cross the Pyrenees which will not become owned by the ancient power. The third child will cause great human suffering, and for a long time the month of March will not be a religious period.*
> *THE EPISTLE TO HENRY II*

Right: The Saint Bernard sanctuary in the Swiss Alps, built to shelter travelers crossing this high mountain pass between Italy and Switzerland.

Opposite: We may well see changes in the nuclear family unit during the next decades.

The eldest child, will, within this interpretation, become involved in Scotland. The arms of Scotland at the time when Nostradamus was alive bore a crowned lion sitting on a crowned helmet with a sword in its paw. (An alternative theory is that she will be active in the province of Nova Scotia, in south-eastern Canada—the St. Lawrence river had been explored by Cartier for France in 1534.)

The second child also looks like having a fairly exciting and far-reaching future, connected with a "Latin" country. In Nostradamus' terms this would either be Latin America or Italy. And as the next reference takes our intrepid second child to Mount Louis we can be fairly sure that Nostradamus was talking about Italy. Mount Louis can be fairly reliably identified as the Great St. Bernard Pass—Mont Louis (the original old French description in Nostradamus' book) refers to the Latin *Mons Jovis,* which in turn refers to the St. Bernard Pass over the Swiss Alps. From here, he will evidently travel from Switzerland through France and across the Pyrenees into the Iberian Peninsula. This area will *not become owned by the ancient power.* Could this refer to a newly independent Basque country, or Catalonia, pointing to a new regional European confederation?

The third child of the future female president, according to our frame of reference, is associated with some adverse influence in the world, which causes suffering in an area connected with religion.

Left: Stonehenge, one of the most ancient and powerfully enigmatic remnants of pagan England.

Opposite: Women's rugby football at Harvard University.

Finally, we hear about the fourth member of the family.

The daughter will become involved with the preservation of the Christian Church. Her husband will fall into contact with religious sects and of her two children, one will remain faithful to the Catholic Church and the other will become involved with a sect.

THE EPISTLE TO HENRY II

Following our logic, it seems that the youngest member of the new president's family will have some influence on the Church. In this case Nostradamus would have been referring to the Catholic Church. We could interpret this quite easily as meaning that this child will perhaps become one of the first female Catholic priests. Nostradamus even goes on to predict that her children will also have religious affiliations,

one to the same Church and the other with what he refers to as a "pagan" sect.

All this might sound somewhat bizarre—it seems unreal to make interpretations such as these about individuals we know little about, people who have not yet achieved fame or impinged upon global consciousness. However, if and when these individuals rise above the "water," so to speak, it will seem totally natural that they should figure in the realm of global affairs.

We have, up to now, interpreted these enigmatic lines in a fairly literal fashion, but if we accept the idea of a feminine influence in the future, a fairly secure assumption, then what we could be looking at is a broader and perhaps more allegorical meaning.

The essence of what Nostradamus is telling us, if we take this seriously, is that there will be a strong alliance between America and Europe which will occur as a result of the presence of a female president.

Right and below: Rock carvings in Sweden of a Neolithic fertility cult.

THE UNITED STATES OF EUROPE

IVEN THAT THE EUROPEAN COMMUNITY has begun the process of attempting to create firm alliances between fourteen nations in the same region, and that this grouping will almost certainly be extended to include a number of other countries—perhaps including the Eastern European and the Baltic nations—it seems likely that this greatly more powerful "nation" of nations will become as powerful as the United States of America.

Given also that we are discussing the rise of the feminine spirit in the future, the ethos of *co-operation* may eventually replace the drive for empowerment or domination. "Super-nations" may perhaps not be so concerned to dominate. They may actually become intelligent for the first time in their long careers, and seek *harmony*. In this case there will be an interim period, while the new paradigm accesses its result, a period when the United States and Europe are courting one another for alliance.

It could be interpreted, therefore, that the new American female president will have a big part to play in this accessing of alliances. Nostradamus may be telling us that we can expect a more formal connection to occur between the United States of America and the European Community which will result in a super-power to beat all super-powers, but in the hands of women, in which case the very concept of "domination" will disappear.

Right: The armed forces of Europe and the United States have deliberately adopted a more flexible policy towards women and children, perhaps with the greater awareness of feminine presence.

In the same sequence from the Epistle to Henry II, Nostradamus gives us further hints to this end.

The other child, who, to his great confusion and late repentance, will want to ruin her, will be involved in three widely different areas, namely the Roman, Germany and Spain, which will arrange different kinds of armed forces.

THE EPISTLE TO HENRY II

The "other child," in our present frame of reference, probably refers to the third child, who caused some consternation in his dealings with the world. He achieves first *confusion*, and then *repentance*, which in Nostradamus' terms is a good process. Within the Catholic tradition, sin followed by repentance is almost better than no sin in the first place! So our third child of the feminine spirit is the prodigal son, who will be active in Italy, Germany and Spain—close to where the second child was traveling across the Alps and the Pyrenees.

Here again, we may wish to abandon the literal interpretation and take hold of the broader, allegorical meaning.

The alliance between the United States and Europe may founder at its start, but then result in something which will provide a new role for the armed forces.

We have, perhaps for some time, been aware of the possibility that the world's armed forces might have a purpose other than that of fighting each other. It may just be that the armies of the major world powers could have the function of helping to keep peace amongst emergent nations.

Left: The Unkillable Human, a sculpture by Frederick Franck. This icon of faith in humanity, dedicated to Sarajevo, was carried there on a peace march in 1994 by group of women from the Dandelion Trust.

Opposite: Ceremony on the completion of a long retreat, Kagyu Buddhist monastery, France.

There is little doubt that the patriarchal attitude of domination by fear will not suddenly disappear with the advent of a critical mass of women in power, and certainly not simply with the arrival of a female American president. So it is clear that the new woman president of the United States will still be dealing with the old values of society, which include the need for armed forces which might help to control troubled nations such as strife-torn Yugoslavia.

What we may be looking at is the feminine influence bringing about a global police authority which will *arrange different kinds of armed forces.*

We may suppose that the sons and daughters of our first female American president are influential in this process.

The story continues:

And everything will pay attention to the ancient religions related to the regions of Europe north of the 48th parallel. These will have trembled to begin with in timidity, but thereafter the areas to the west, south and east will also tremble. But the nature of their power will be such that co-operation will work better than war.

One of the most convincing aspects of Nostradamus' prophecies is the fact that there is such consistency within and between the different works. It may not seem so to the casual reader, but once the verses and writings of this extraordinary prophet are examined in more detail, there arise numerous instances when one part of the work backs up another.

This is the case in these lines. First of all we hear again the word "co-operation," which we may take to signal a complete change in attitude. Second we learn that there is an important influence in the form of ancient religions, as we had learned before when Nostradamus told us of "pagan" religions and sects. It may be fair to suggest that as the organized religious belief systems become less reliable, and as people turn more to the personal side of religion—as is already happening in the late twentieth century, when cult religions have offered more, and freer, possibilities than for a long time—so small, "cult-type" religious belief systems will grow in popularity.

But the nature of their power will be such that co-operation will work better than war.

This is perhaps the most significant line in the whole piece—that there will be attempts to resolve differences through co-operation rather than conflict.

If the new female president achieves this, she will have done more than any past male president of the United States.

To sum up the story so far, according to this interpretation of the Epistle to Henry II:

  ❨   We can expect to see a female candidate win the United States presidential election in the year 2000.

  ❨   This individual may be Ann Richards, Barbara Boxer or another female candidate living in the south of the country.

  ❨   Whoever she is, her four offspring will play a major part in the world's political and religious future, in particular in relation to a stronger alliance between the United States and Europe.

  ❨   This may also be seen as an allegorical presentation of the furtherance of the feminist movement in the United States and Europe, where these four individuals play a determining role in the way that human relations improve.

  ❨   A world policing force will grow out of the United States-Europe alliance. And as a result of this new view of politics, co-operation will be a key word.

  ❨   Mainstream religion will take a greater account of small sect-oriented belief systems.

  ❨   And, to be remembered from an earlier chapter, the female presidency will run into problems around three decades after it has begun, say in the beginning of the third decade of the twenty-first century.

All this will occur from about 1996, through 2000, and up to approximately the year 2030.

7

ANTICHRISTS
AND PLAGUES

TWO OF NOSTRADAMUS' FAVORITE SUBJECTS, other than the constant presence of war, are the Antichrists who will visit the world and the plagues that will reduce it.

It must be said that throughout the centuries since Nostradamus made his strange and often eccentric prophecies, there has been almost nothing other than war and disease. The world is beset by suffering brought about by conflicts between nations and religions, and as if this were not enough, disease has continuously manifested itself in different forms, ranging from the black death (or pestilence) to cancer and now AIDS. It is therefore not surprising that Nostradamus pays so much attention to these areas of life.

One of the ways he focuses on war is through the reporting of a number of what he calls "Antichrists." These are particularly evil individuals who have held, and will continue to hold, sway over mankind in one form or another to its disadvantage. The first Antichrist he predicted was Napoleon, the second was Hitler, and we can evidently, according to many interpretations, expect the third sometime soon. His name is sometimes given as Mabus, but as the authors pointed out in a previous volume on Nostradamus, this character might actually be not an individual, but a place and a time.

In any event, according to further lines in the Epistle to Henry II, developing the theme of the emergent feminist powers, the new woman president and her literal or allegorical offspring will come into contact with this third Antichrist and with the damage he may be able to inflict on the world. The following lines take up the story.

> *Then the great Empire of the Antichrist will begin where Attila's empire once existed, and the new Xerxes will arrive with many followers, so that the coming of the Holy Spirit from the area of the 48th degree will see a transmigration which will chase away the abomination of this Antichrist, who will make war on the Royal Pope and the Christian Church, and whose reign will continue until the end of time....*

> *...Then will commence a persecution of the Churches the like of which was never seen before. And at the same time a great plague will grow so that more than two thirds of the world will be gone.*
> THE EPISTLE TO HENRY II

This so-called third Antichrist has been the subject of much debate, largely because it is fair to assume from reading the relevant verses in the *Centuries* that Nostradamus got the first two right. (He prophesied in code the advent of Napoleon, and actually gave a name that was close enough to Hitler—"Hister"—to identify

him precisely.) We do not want another Hitler, for sure, so there have been many attempts to identify the third candidate for the title *before* he emerges, presumably because we imagine that we might be able to stop him causing too much harm that way.

Various interpreters have concluded from Nostradamus' verses that this individual will be born in Egypt or the Middle East with two teeth in the back of his throat. It is said that he will conquer the world with love—this would perhaps make him a strange Antichrist, but not necessarily a strange anti-Christian—gathering millions of followers who will be intoxicated by his leadership and charisma. It is said that he will cause immense difficulties to the governments of the major powers, but that they will eventually manage to kill him.

These interpretations of him do not necessarily lead us to believe that he is bad, in the sense of being anti-human, but that he may simply not be what the major powers and leaders of society want—given that he will probably stand for opposing principles.

According to the lines above, this third Antichrist will be "the big one." He will be the one who brings an almost world-wide revolution.

And to make matters worse, the next lines tell us that a massive plague, probably, it is believed, AIDS,

Below: Sculpture in Oslo, by Gustav Vigeland.

will wipe out large parts of the world's population at the same period of time.

Nostradamus actually gives an indication of when all this doom and disaster will occur—around the time of a major solar eclipse, which he tells us will be *more dark and gloomy than any other since the creation of the world...* But then he adds: *...except that after the death and passion of Jesus Christ.*

It would seem from all this that we are looking at a time of great stress for the governments of the world, including that of our female president of the United States. The text continues:

At the eve of another desolation, when she is atop her most high and sublime dignity, some potentates and warlords confront her and take away her weapons, leaving her only the insignia of her power, whose shape attracts them.

It has to be said that, in the context of the rest of the Epistle to Henry II, there is no certainty that this "she" refers to the female president of the United States or indeed to the feminist principle as a whole, but there are sufficient indications to suggest that it might. The proposed interpretation is consistent with the time-line established in Chapter Two and with the prediction which tells us that after a period of time (eighteen years) the feminine movement will founder and troubles will cause it to transform itself. The lines above suggest that a great power will lose its strength and become merely an figurehead.

Certainly it is not hard to predict the likelihood that the AIDS virus, unless cured before the end of this century, will kill many more millions of people around the world than we are currently willing to anticipate. This will be perhaps the single most terrible problem that our female president will face in the twenty-first century.

THE END OF FEAR

Eyes closed, opened by antique imagination,
The habits of those alone will be brought to nothing:
The great monarch will chastise their frenzy,
Attacking the treasures before the temples.

The body without soul no longer to be sacrificed:
Deaths day will be birthday:
The divine spirit will make the soul happy,
Seeing the word in its eternity.

CENTURY 2: 11-12

ONE OF THE MOST IMPORTANT TRANSFORMING POWERS of the women's movement, which is of great value to the future, is the ability to end fear.

If there is one aspect of the patriarchal system that has done the greatest damage, it is the engendering of an almost inherent fearfulness within us all.

We are not talking about the kind of fear which causes us to jump out of the way of a speeding car, or avoid contact with an angry lion. This is not so much fear as the need to survive—a kind of physical reflex which arises from a million years of conditioning.

The fear we are discussing here is the existential fear which arises in the absence of love or light. For thousands of years now we have been under the influence of religions which are essentially fear-driven: Christianity, Judaism, Islam, Hinduism. If you are sinful you will not go to heaven. If you do not obey the law

Below: *The River of Life.* Pen and water-color drawing by the English visionary William Blake, c. 1805.

you will be destroyed. If you behave in a certain "evil" way during this life, you will suffer during the next.

The original concept behind these absurd ideas was to help people whose lives were disastrously unhappy anyway. If you lived in huts or tents or on the street, and had no food to eat, no one who loved you, no place to go, these religions provided you with something simple to keep you going. There was a prospect of "heaven," even if it was only after death. At least there was something to hope for. If you lived without sin (whatever that is) you might be happy after you die. But now, thousands of years after all this was created, we still think in terms of being "God-fearing," as though this were a good thing. And this God-fearing attitude colors all aspects of our lives.

After thousands of years of conditioning, we believe in this punitive God on a level which we can no longer access or change. Essentially what this belief has done is to put out the light, leaving us mostly in the dark. The underlying basis for it is redundant in most Western countries because now we have luxury, most of us are loved by someone, we live regular, secure lives, and have often the opportunity to live in heaven right now, if we could just stop complaining for a moment. But still we carry this unconscious fear around with us as though it were essential to our lives. It takes the form of continuous worrying, fear of losing control of our lives, fear of tomorrow, fear of losing the job, the girlfriend, the house, fear of death.

As the patriarchal "atmosphere" disperses with the arrival of a critical mass of women, so basic and essential aspects of our lives will be transformed. This is why it is so important that women become our political leaders, our religious leaders, our mother goddesses again.

We began Chapter Six with a single verse which told us about the order that will result in the next century from the arrival of a greater feminine spirit. This quatrain is followed by three more which continue the story, two of which are set out at the beginning of this prediction. There follows now a free interpretation of all four verses.

Before long everything will be rearranged. We can expect a very strange century. Women's estate that was masked and alone will change everything. Few will wish to remain the way they were.

The next son of the important one will become powerful in the realm of the privileged and everyone will be afraid of his greed. But his disciples will be thrown out.

Opposite: His Holiness the Fourteenth Dalai Lama of Tibet, one of the most important living teachers of the new religious awareness.

Eyes that were closed will be opened by an ancient understanding. The aura and environment of those who have been alone will be proven pointless, and the religious leaders and those that have an investment in continuing fear will chastise the enthusiasm of the rest, putting the newfound treasure down as useless.

It will be shown that the body is not important because the soul always continues, and death will be regarded as the same as birth. The understanding that the spirit is divine will make everyone joyful, because they will see the truth on a broader level.

This is no mean piece of prophecy, and exemplifies the extraordinary capability and understanding of this enigmatic man. The story he tells us is of the arrival of a new force which has hitherto been masked. We are interpreting this as meaning women's estate, and that upon the arrival of this estate everything will be reordered and everyone will quickly realize what problems had previously been caused by patriarchy. Life is like that. We have a tendency to labor on in conditions which are not ideal because we cannot conceive of anything different. We complain continuously, but do nothing to change the situation. And then something happens and we find ourselves in a new situation which is better for us. What a relief! If only it had happened earlier.

Such is the change which Nostradamus describes. But a major part of this transformation is that we learn to throw out the old habits and adopt a new approach.

And that new way is religious, as is so much of our fundamental nature.

Eyes that were closed will be opened by an ancient understanding....

Ancient religious understanding is already gaining greater importance than it has had for centuries. In the United States and some European countries, paganism, or neo-paganism, has become so popular that there are even sects that have adopted the ancient ideals of natural harmony, love of the environment, the ancient goddesses, and brought them to the forefront again. These old understandings will become new again, according to our prophet.

Nostradamus next uses the fear surrounding loneliness as his metaphor for the change. What he is telling us is that we will not need to fear being alone, or unloved, because the new belief systems of the feminine order will help everyone to accept the human condition in its real and natural form. There are already many groups of people gathering together to take advantage, for example, of the Buddhist philosophies which are so much more supportive of human nature, and less concerned to be critical of sexual

attitudes and needs—aspects of human nature that have been put down so vehemently by the Christian faiths. There are also numerous smaller religious groups, which we may choose to call cults, which are creating new ways of living based on ancient religions from the East. All this is part of the change that humanity so badly needs.

The traditional religious leaders will attempt to dampen the new spirit, but this will not succeed. And in the last lines we get the point of it all:

It will be shown that the body is not important because the soul always continues, and death will be regarded as the same as birth. The understanding that the spirit is divine will make everyone joyful, because they will see the truth on a broader level.

Essentially we shall discover that life is eternal, and there is nothing to stop us all being joyful NOW. That we do not need to fear death because it is only another life transition, and if we do not fear death then there is no need to worry about what tomorrow will bring.

Perhaps all this sounds hugely idealistic and too hopeful, but maybe the future really could be a better place, and our pessimism only arises out of the patriarchal conditioning that we have suffered for so long.

MOVING THE STARS AND THE POPE

The great star will burn for seven days,
The cloud will cause two suns to appear:
A great howling will be heard from morning to night
When the great pontiff will change country.

CENTURY 2: 14

DURING THE SUMMER OF 1994 some twenty-one meteorites crashed into the planet Jupiter, with a force thousands of times greater than any nuclear bomb. The effect on Earth was minimal because Jupiter is far, far away. But the very fact of the bombardment made a major impact, inasmuch as if it can happen there it can also happen here.

The military and NASA in the United States have already begun planning ways of pre-empting a meteorite "attack." How they would stop twenty-one of them is hard to conceive, especially if they happened to be several hundred miles across, as some of those that hit Jupiter were.

Nevertheless, the concept of our planet's being vulnerable to something other than itself is encouraging, for it changes the attitude of those who live upon it in the same way as going to the Moon did in the 1960s. And this is the point of the verse at the top of the page.

We are told of a great star burning for seven days. Previous interpreters have related this to a nuclear bomb, but there is little likelihood of any nuclear device burning for such a long time. A meteorite rushing towards the planet, however, could well be seen for seven days before impact. The second line informs us of a cloud exposing two suns. This could

imply that it later becomes evident that there are two meteorites on the horizon.

Next we are given a description of the commotion this will make—a howling sound that continues from morning till night. And finally, the whole prediction is put into the context of the Pope changing country.

What do we make of all this?

The straightforward interpretation of this quatrain is that a meteorite bombardment will occur after a warning of seven days. Two meteorites will hit the Earth, and the timing of this will coincide with the movement of the Pope from Rome.

As we have not already seen these events coincide—a meteorite hitting the Earth and the moving of the papacy—it can only be presumed that this will happen in the future.

Nostradamus made detailed prophecies about the changes associated with the women's movement, including the election of a female American president which will presage the coming to power of other women in other parts of the world. Given all this, we may be sure that one of the likeliest candidates for change will be the Catholic Church.

We have already discussed the expectation of the rise of new cult religions, of a return to holistic pagan beliefs based on natural harmony with our planet. We have seen that the various organized religions of the world will not be able to resist much longer the growing presence of women in their ranks. And we have accepted perhaps the prophecy that patriarchal society cannot continue much longer.

Given all this, we might well imagine the possibility of a relocated pope. There are a number of

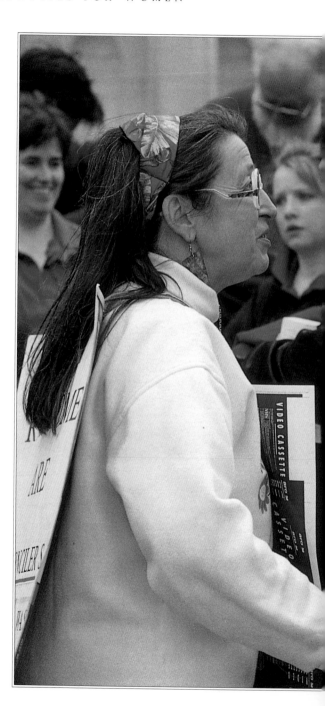

Right: Encounter during a demonstration, at London's Westminster Cathedral, in April 1994, for the ordination of women priests within the Catholic Church.

specific predictions which tell us of the problems the Church will experience towards the end of the millennium. We sampled one of them in Chapter Three under the heading "Women and God." This foretold a major transformation in the substance of the Church of Rome.

Another verse reads as follows:

> *Shortly before the monarch is assassinated,*
> *Castor and Pollux in the ship with a bearded star:*
> *The public fund emptied by land and sea,*
> *Pisa, Asti, Ferrara, Turin land under order.*
> CENTURY 2: 15

In Greek mythology, Castor and Pollux, the heavenly twins, were the protectors of seamen. In this context they represent Saints Peter and Paul, and their ship the Catholic Church. The bearded star is a comet or meteorite, traditionally an evil omen, and the conjunction of these emblems portends difficulties for the Church in uncharted waters. We can relate this reference to the expected changes in the general condition of organized religion throughout the "civilized" world.

We could say that the whole of history has been a series of wars and cataclysms, but surely the end of this millennium has seen a much higher instance of

wars, earthquakes, and other natural disasters, than any other period in history. It is as though we are building up to an apocalypse, a massive and critical change that will bring about a total transformation of the human race in the years to come. And this verse is yet another part of the puzzle.

The formula works approximately as follows:

The critical mass of the feminine spirit =
the depletion of patriarchy =
chaos and change in religion, industry, politics
+ the instance of natural catastrophes =
further transformation =
eventual freedom from the repression of the past.

We might reduce this for the sake of simplicity to the following:

Woman brings man to balance,
brings the world to justice and truth.

And still further simplified:

Woman + Man = Truth.

Ultimately, whether he was fully aware of what he was predicting or not, Nostradamus understood intuitively that this would be the result of a growth in the power of the feminine principle.

CELEBRATIONS IN LONDON

*A*ND THE STORY CONTINUES in the following verses. Nostradamus very often wrote his quatrains in sequence, rather like a map of our future. In the section entitled "The End of Fear," the passages (Century 2: 10-13) revealed the possibility of a new understanding of life and death.

These lines were followed by a verse describing the transformation of the Catholic Church, which we discussed in the last section, "Moving the Stars and the Pope." Two verses after this we find the following:

Naples, Palermo, Sicily, Syracuse,
New leaders, celestial lightning and fires,
Power from London, Ghent, Brussels and Susa,
Great slaughter, triumph leads to festivities.
CENTURY 2: 16

It is suggested that this quatrain prophesies a collective response to a meteorite attack—that the combined military forces of many nations manage to stop or destroy the two massive rocks that were hurtling towards the planet, "slaughtering" them, and that this triumph leads to great celebrations.

This, on the face of it, shows us a great victory. But on a more subtle level it is a victory of a different kind. The world's military might would, in this case, have been used for the benefit of mankind, not to its disadvantage. Armies and weapons would have been employed to save humanity from death, rather than cause it.

This would be a cause for celebration. And certainly such a transformation would have a direct connection with a greater feminine presence in positions of political and religious power.

The military activity caused by the imminent arrival of two massive meteorites seems to center on southern Italy, north Africa, and other areas of Europe, including London and Ghent, Belgium, the country where the European Community has its administration. Interestingly, in Nostradamus' day, control of the Sultanate of Susa, in Tunisia, was being contested by Hapsburg Spain and the advancing Ottoman Empire. So we are being shown the rival worlds of Christendom and Islam uniting to triumph over an extraterrestrial threat.

THE STRENGTH OF WEAKNESS

ONTINUING IN THE SAME VEIN, we find another verse in this sequence which gives us a prediction of the natural conse-quence of a new view of co-operation—the disbanding of armies in a future governed by women.

The aimless army of Europe will depart,
Joining together close to the submerged island:
The weakened fleet will fold up,
At the navel of the world, a greater voice replacing it.

CENTURY 2:22

There are two indications in this quatrain which, in the light of earlier verses, specifically place it in our immediate future. One of Nostradamus' earlier verses makes a famous prediction, which has been echoed by other prophets, including the modern American prophet Edgar Cayce. In this prophecy, part of England's south coast will sink into the sea because of a geological change. Nostradamus refers again to that prediction here. Cayce specifically states that this will occur at the end of the twentieth century or the beginning of the twenty-first.

Also, the last line of this verse repeats the prediction that the Pope will change locations—*At the navel of the world, a greater voice replacing it.* The "navel of the world" is probably an allegorical reference to Rome as the religious center of the world (at least from the perspective of Nostradamus' age).

Below: Harmony in the Garden of Eden; detail of Brueghel's *Paradiso.*

Opposite: Generations at play. Grandmother and grandson playing football on the beach.

Previous page: Sister Mary Chantal kicking back at an opponent in a martial arts class, New York City, 1994.
Page 197: Halley's Comet, thought to be an ill omen, terrifies the people in 1066. King Harold of England is warned of the impending Norman invasion. Bayeux Tapestry, France.
Page 196: The tower of Big Ben at the Houses of Parliament in London.

So we are placing this event, concerning the European army, at approximately the same time as all the other events that are occurring because of the presence of a female American president and the greater power of the feminine spirit.

And the prediction is telling us that because of a lack of energy, an aimlessness, the European army will cease to exist and the weakened fleet (the Navy) will also fold up and pack its bags. And all this will come about because there is an overriding cause— *a greater voice replacing it.*

This general demobilization could, of course, be connected with the alliance we spoke of earlier between the United States and Europe, in which armies are redeployed to police the world. It could also flow from the experience of joint action in the face of external threat to the planet. It certainly suggests that in the future there will be less need for armies because wars will no longer be a regular event.

Whatever the cause, the result must be good. The fewer armies the better.

DISAVOWING THE OLD HABITS

N ATURALLY, WITH THE DEVELOPMENT of a completely new paradigm, many of the old habits will become redundant. Some of us may rue the day that our "normal" lives are disrupted, others will cheer that ancient, tired and bored behavior will be replaced with something fresh. This is another of the characteristics of women—that they invar-iably cause the world to have to change. Once put into positions of power in greater numbers there will be no standing still, even for a moment.

And one of these changes is outlined in a strange, enigmatic verse:

> *When the adulterer who is wounded*
> *without a blow being struck,*
> *he will have murdered his wife and son*
> *out of frustration:*
> *wife knocked over he will strangle the child.*
> CENTURY 8: 63

This piece of prophecy is one of those found scattered throughout the writings of Nostradamus which we might call "prophecies of general change." Put another way, they appear, usually as single verses, as though Nostradamus were simply commenting by the wayside. Traveling along through the events of the centuries, he pauses every so often to make a general comment about conditions of life at some particular moment. This verse seems to tell us something about the state of marriage and its effect on the family unit.

Right: Father and son. New, flexible family arrangements will replace the rigidities of traditional social roles.

As the feminine spirit moves forward during the next century, entirely different conditions will evolve. Once women are no longer forced -through their parents' ideas and conditioning—to become wives, family makers and mothers, but are free to choose whether to do this or not, the whole family structure will have to change. Women may still wish to stay at home and raise children, but they may also wish to bear children and have the men stay at home and father them. This is already happening in the latter years of the twentieth century, but in future it will become even more common, affecting the way we see our marital structures.

There may even be happier and more fulfilling ways for children to be born. Once we have finally broken free of all the complications attendant on organized religion, and become practical about life and death, the mores surrounding marriage and birth will be transformed into something more realistic. We may abandon the idea of marriage as a religious vow altogether. This is not to say that people will not continue to be married—if that makes us happy, why not? But already, during this century, the estate of marriage has changed dramatically because of the greatly increased instance of divorce. For many of us marriage is no more than a romantic idea, and does not need to become a prison.

Below: The nuclear family unit could do with some repairs, or perhaps even a total overhaul—protesters against family violence.

Opposite: A couple preparing for natural childbirth at home.

Overleaf: Colored engraving of Nostradamus. French, seventeenth century.

In the verse we are looking at here, Nostradamus suggests that adultery and marriage have wounded the heart—*wounded without a blow being struck*—and that the man, through frustration "murders" the wife and child. This could be seen to be a description of how families can develop into states of pain and violence.

But as we have seen, it is now possible for women to stand up and be heard on the often tender and painful subject of family problems. As we have mentioned in an earlier chapter, television programs such as the Oprah Winfrey Show have given women a voice, and the knowledge that their voice is actually being listened to and acted upon. This has been immensely valuable in the evolution of the feminine spirit and will lead to women refusing to accept what they are hurt by, and refusing to be dominated by frustrated and poorly conditioned men. In turn, men will change their attitudes towards women, and many of the old prejudices will begin to disappear.

THE PROPHET'S VISION

HAT WE FIND IN NOSTRADAMUS' OVERALL VISION of the future of women during the next two decades is a radical paradigm shift in the quality of life, brought about by a much stronger and more revolutionary movement on the part of women than might have been expected during our times.

There is a tendency amongst conservative male groups to suggest that the feminist movement has been militant enough, and that men are already changing to accommodate the demands of women. But Nostradamus indicates that the movement has hardly even begun. It is natural, as we have seen, for the habit of patriarchy to stick. It is also normal for a very considerable critical mass to be needed to shift anything that has been an established habit for so long. We could not have expected, for example, to change the attitudes of certain groups of white people towards black people, or the entrenched prejudice against homosexual love, without major upheaval. These changes are still occurring, and have had to pass through long periods of difficulty for the paradigm shift to occur. But the patriarchal prejudice against the feminine is older and far more entrenched, being the result of millennia of thoughtless violence and suppression.

We can expect, therefore, a great deal more upheaval associated with feminism, and the balance of power between the sexes, than we have hitherto experienced. And if we believe in Nostradamus' capacity to predict the future, the first major move to this end will be the Seline March, which will occur during the winter of the year that the comet Chiron is visible from Earth. This will be followed by the greater political presence of a certain woman in American political life, and her election in the millennial year.

Nostradamus prophesies that humanity will be led thereafter into a happier and more harmonious future, flowing from an acceptance of the rightful place of the feminine in all our lives.

CONCLUSION

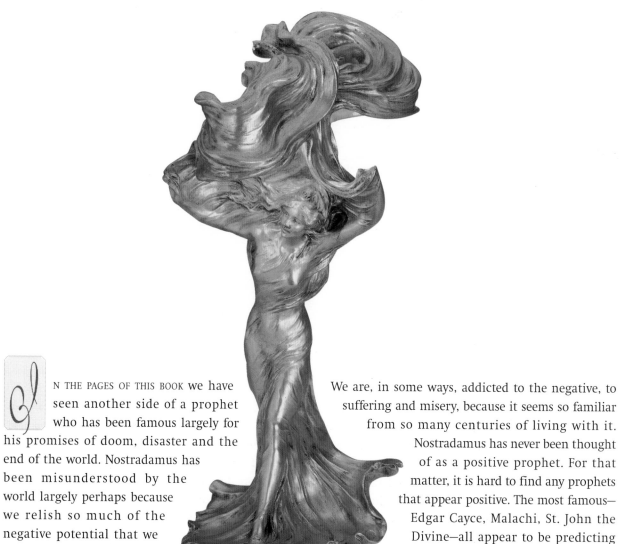

*O*N THE PAGES OF THIS BOOK we have seen another side of a prophet who has been famous largely for his promises of doom, disaster and the end of the world. Nostradamus has been misunderstood by the world largely perhaps because we relish so much of the negative potential that we believe lies in our future.

We are, in some ways, addicted to the negative, to suffering and misery, because it seems so familiar from so many centuries of living with it. Nostradamus has never been thought of as a positive prophet. For that matter, it is hard to find any prophets that appear positive. The most famous— Edgar Cayce, Malachi, St. John the Divine—all appear to be predicting doom of one sort or another.

Below: Roots by Frida Kahlo, 1943.

Opposite: Art Nouveau sculpture of the American dancer Loie Fuller, *c.* 1900, by Raoul Larche.

But Nostradamus' works are so large and far-reaching that if we look a little more closely, and read perhaps a little more between the lines, we begin to make discoveries of secret treasures that would never have been apparent to us at a simple glance.

His works contain a mass of material related to love, marriage, relationships, women, changes in society—matters far removed from war or disaster. In fact, if we look at some of the verses that have been interpreted as being connected to doom and disaster—to the bigger events of history—we find that they can just as well to apply to simpler, smaller matters. We discover, to our surprise, that very often they don't relate at all to what we have believed them to be about.

It all comes from our perspective. It derives from our conditioning, from what our expectations are. There are no sure facts about Nostradamus, or any other prophet. Much of what the great prophets wrote was intended to reflect the age in which it was interpreted, and if we read the later writings of Nostradamus, letters and notes which preceded his death, we find clear comments on how the twentieth century would be an age when people would begin to realize the value of predicting the future as a device for changing it.

The predominant role of womankind in the future of humanity, according to twentieth-century understanding, is as essential to our development as the former dominance of men was. Mankind, according to Nostradamus, has worked in a masculine way to build and initiate, to create a life of human values out of the raw material of planet Earth. The need for women to become more powerful is part of the process of transcendence, a greater and higher function of human nature. Women in the future are needed to soften the harshness that male energy has produced on Earth, to provide a greater measure of love and wisdom, something that mankind has often lacked in the past.

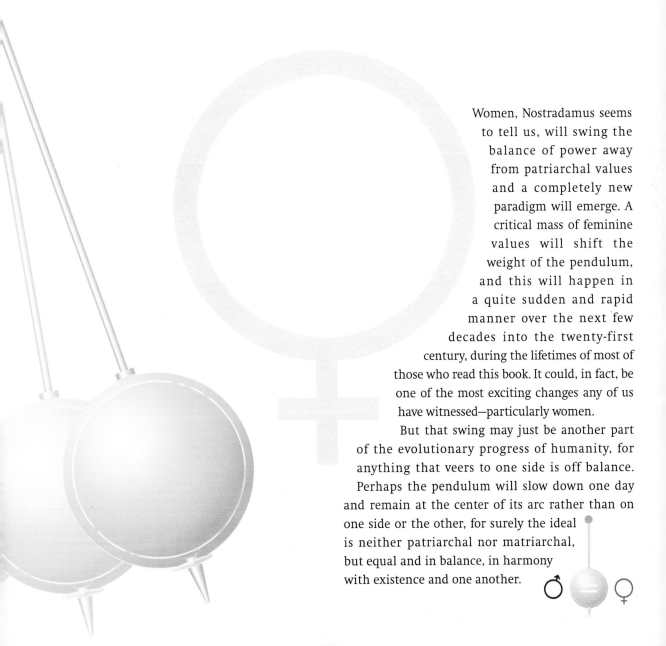

Women, Nostradamus seems to tell us, will swing the balance of power away from patriarchal values and a completely new paradigm will emerge. A critical mass of feminine values will shift the weight of the pendulum, and this will happen in a quite sudden and rapid manner over the next few decades into the twenty-first century, during the lifetimes of most of those who read this book. It could, in fact, be one of the most exciting changes any of us have witnessed—particularly women.

But that swing may just be another part of the evolutionary progress of humanity, for anything that veers to one side is off balance. Perhaps the pendulum will slow down one day and remain at the center of its arc rather than on one side or the other, for surely the ideal is neither patriarchal nor matriarchal, but equal and in balance, in harmony with existence and one another.

Terracotta relief of Lilith, the demonic Mesopotamian goddess of the night, c. 2000 B.C. In Hebrew legend she was the first bride of Adam, cast out and cursed for refusing to submit to him.

he original work of Michel de Nostradame was entitled the *Centuries*. This consisted of ten volumes of cryptic prophecies written in verse form, with nearly a 1000 verses.

Nostradamus' verses are very difficult to understand and even more difficult to interpret as "sensible" prophecies relating to our future. There are a number of modern editions in print with commentaries by interpreters such as Erika Cheetham and Henry C. Roberts. The following are among the best.

Cheetham, Erika. *The Prophecies of Nostradamus.* London: Spearman, 1933, and various paperback editions.

Hogue, John. *Nostradamus and the Millennium.* New York: Doubleday Books, 1987.

Leoni, Edgar. *Nostradamus and His Prophecies.* New York: Bell, 1982.

Lorie, Peter. *Nostradamus — The Millennium and Beyond.* New York: Simon & Schuster, 1993.

Roberts, Henry C. *The Complete Prophecies of Nostradamus.* London: Harper Collins, 1985, and various paperback editions.

B O O K S O N W O M E N ' S I S S U E S

Aburdene, Patricia & John Naisbitt. *Megatrends for Women.* London: Random House, 1993.

Eisler, Riane. *The Chalice and the Blade.* San Francisco: HarperSanFrancisco, 1988.

French, Marilyn. *Beyond Power,* London: Jonathan Cape, 1985.

Partnow, Elaine. *The New Quotable Woman.* London: Headline, 1993.

Sjöö, Monica & Barbara Mor. *The Great Cosmic Mother — Rediscovering the Religion of the Earth.* San Francisco: Harper & Row, 1987.

Wolf, Naomi. *Fire with Fire.* London: Chatto & Windus, Random House, 1993.

ACKNOWLEDGMENTS

Selected excerpts from *The Great Cosmic Mother*, by Monica Sjöö and Barbara Mor.
Copyright © 1987 by Barbara Mor and Monica Sjöö.
Reprinted by permission of HarperCollins Publishers, Inc.: page 75.

The Chalice And The Blade: Our History, Our Future, by Riane Eisler.
HarperCollins Publishers Inc., 1993: pages 104, 156.

Fire With Fire, by Naomi Wolf. Reprinted by permission of Random House Inc., 1993: pages 88, 93, 161.

Megatrends For Women, by Patricia Aburdene and John Naisbitt.
Reprinted by permission of Random House Inc., 1993: pages 53, 78, 79, 96, 112, 131, 160.

Beyond Power, by Marilyn French. Copyright © 1985 by Belles-Lettres, Inc.
For North America, reprinted by permission of Simon & Schuster, Inc.
For UK and Commonwealth rights, reprinted by permission of Jonathan Cape.
Both editions 1985. Pages 9, 29, 159.

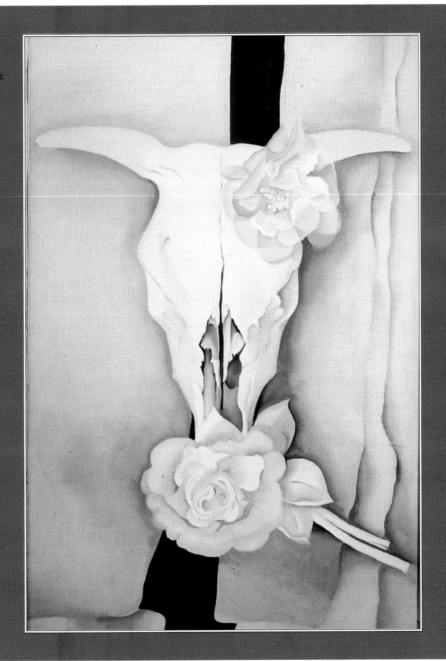

Right: Cow's Skull with Calico Roses. Painting by Georgia O'Keeffe.

Overleaf: Fearless futures. Six-month-old babies learning to swim.

221